THIS BOOK BELONGS TO

START DATE

| MONTH | DAY | YEAR |

EDITORIAL

EDITORS-IN-CHIEF
Raechel Myers & Amanda Bible Williams

CONTENT DIRECTOR
Russ Ramsey, MDiv., ThM.

MANAGING EDITOR
Jessica Lamb

EDITOR
Kara Gause

CREATIVE

CREATIVE DIRECTOR
Ryan Myers

ART DIRECTOR
Amanda Barnhart

DESIGNER
Kelsea Allen

PRODUCTION DESIGNER
Julie Allen

COVER PHOTOGRAPHER
Rachael Baxter

PHOTOGRAPHERS
Michael Matti
Carter Moore
Raechel Myers
Raj Nair
Paul Tellefsen
Jared Whitney
Amanda Bible Williams
Jonathan Zoeteman

@SHEREADSTRUTH

SHEREADSTRUTH.COM

SUBSCRIPTION INQUIRIES
orders@shereadstruth.com

SHE READS TRUTH™

© 2017 by She Reads Truth, LLC

All rights reserved.

ISBN 978-1-946282-32-3

All Scripture is taken from the Christian Standard Bible®, Copyright © 2017 by Holman Bible Publishers. Used by permission. Christian Standard Bible® and CSB® are federally registered trademarks of Holman Bible Publishers.

Verses omitted in the CSB are also omitted in this book.

This book was printed offset in Nashville, Tennessee, on 70# Lynx Opaque. Cover is 100# Cougar Opaque with a soft touch lamination.

Matthew: This Is Jesus

"Who is Jesus?"

They all asked the question. Those who walked the streets with Jesus, who encountered His teaching in the synagogues, who witnessed Him healing the sick and eating with sinners—they were compelled to know who this man was. That was 2,000 years ago. Yet here we are, asking the same question today.

Even now, sitting in my Nashville office, surrounded by modern technology and Western comforts, I can think of no more foundational question to ask. The answer frames what I believe about God. It frames what I know about myself and how I view the world around me. And, on one hand, my response as a Christian is simple: Jesus is the Son of God. But because that is true, is there not infinitely more to know?

Theologian Charles Hodge said, "The gospel is so simple that small children can understand it, and it is so profound that studies by the wisest theologians will never exhaust its riches." I believe he's right, and I believe the same is true with the central figure of that gospel, the person of Jesus Christ. We cannot exhaust the depth of who He is, but we can know Him. The Gospel of Matthew is a great place to start.

> **"**
>
> *In telling us who Jesus is, Matthew tells the story of our salvation*

Beginning with a genealogy, Matthew lays out his account of who Jesus is: the Messiah that the Jewish people—and the world—had been waiting for. He presents Jesus as the Son of God, born of the Holy Spirit, baptized by a prophet, and tempted by the devil. He shows Jesus as teacher, healer, servant, and friend—a man who walked the earth but was not bound by it. In telling us who Jesus is, Matthew tells the story of our salvation.

Think of this study book as your guide to Matthew's Gospel, created to introduce you not only to the text itself, but also to the people and places you'll encounter as you read. Key names and people groups are called out and defined as you make your way through, and a map in the margins will help you track where the various stories happened in proximity to one another. Each special feature you come across is designed to orient you to the land Jesus walked, the truth He taught, and the people who played a part in the story.

As you read, check in occasionally with the "Who Is Jesus?" chart on page 130. It's my favorite feature in the book because it reminds me of the true answers to that all-important question. Jesus is the Son of God. He is the Savior, the Christ, the Messiah.

This is the story Matthew tells. This is Jesus.

Read on.

Amanda

Amanda Bible Williams
EDITOR-IN-CHIEF

"

We formatted this book a little bit like a textbook...

Every time our team creates a study book, we want content to drive design, and design to direct the reader back to Scripture.

Because the Gospel of Matthew presents the true history and message of Jesus's life, we formatted this book a little bit like a textbook, explaining names, locations, and people groups as Matthew introduces them.

Our team scattered educational resources throughout this book more than any other book we've designed, including our favorite set of spreads, "The 12 Disciples," on pages 24–27.

Using photos from our team's recent trip to Israel, alongside other modern-day photos of the region, we were able to give visual context to the places Matthew mentions in his Gospel. (Our favorite is our Editor-in-Chief Amanda's shot of the Mount of Beatitudes with the Sea of Galilee in the background on page 33.)

We hope these details, along with subtle touches like color-coded wayfinding tabs for each week and the personal touch of handwritten day titles, will invite you into God's living and active Word.

Enjoy *Matthew: This Is Jesus*—inherently beautiful words, intentionally designed to meet you today.

THE SHE READS TRUTH CREATIVE TEAM

She Reads Truth is a community of women dedicated to reading the Word of God every day. The Bible is living and active, breathed out by God, and we confidently hold it higher than anything we can do or say. This book focuses primarily on Scripture, with bonus resources to facilitate deeper engagement with God's Word.

SCRIPTURE READING

This study book presents the book of Matthew in daily readings, plus supplementary passages for additional context and tools to help you gain a deeper understanding of Matthew's Gospel.

DIG DEEPER

Each weekday includes three simple prompts to help you process and respond to the daily reading.

GRACE DAY

Use this day of the week to pray, rest, and reflect on what you've read.

For added community and conversation, join us in the **Matthew** reading plan on the She Reads Truth app or at SheReadsTruth.com.

WEEKLY TRUTH

This day is set aside for weekly Scripture memorization.

Find the corresponding memory card in the back of your book.

ON THE TIMELINE:

Matthew was written in the first century, around AD 60, before the fall of the temple in Jerusalem in AD 70. The events of Matthew took place during the life of Christ, between roughly 5 BC and AD 33.

A LITTLE BACKGROUND:

Though he did not identify himself in the text, the early Church unanimously affirmed that the Gospel of Matthew was authored by the apostle Matthew. Most scholars believe that Matthew used Mark's Gospel in writing his own. If this is correct, Matthew's Gospel was written after Mark's, though the date of Mark's Gospel is also a bit of a mystery. Irenaeus (approx. AD 180) claimed that Mark wrote his Gospel after Peter's death in the mid-60s. However, Clement of Alexandria, who wrote only twenty years after Irenaeus, claimed that Mark wrote his Gospel while Peter was still alive.

MESSAGE AND PURPOSE:

It seems fitting that the first book of the New Testament begins with the words: "An account of the genealogy of Jesus Christ." This Gospel was written from a strong Jewish perspective to show that Jesus truly is the Messiah and coming King promised in the Old Testament.

Matthew presents an eyewitness testimony of the ministry of Jesus and emphasizes certain theological truths:

Jesus is the Messiah, the long-awaited King of God's people.

Jesus is the new Abraham, the founder of a new spiritual Israel consisting of all people (both Jews and Gentiles) who follow Him.

Jesus is the new Moses, the deliverer, instructor, and mediator of God's people.

Jesus is the Immanuel, the virgin-born Son of God who fulfills the promises of the Old Testament.

GIVE THANKS FOR THE GOSPEL OF MATTHEW:

As the first book in the New Testament, the Gospel of Matthew serves as a gateway between the Old and New Testaments. Of the New Testament books, and certainly of the four Gospels, Matthew also makes the most direct connections to the Old Testament. The book presents God's entire plan of salvation from Genesis to Revelation, referring to Old Testament prophecies about sixty times. Matthew looks forward by discussing not only the Messiah's coming and His ministry, but also His future plan for His Church and kingdom.

Repent BECAUSE THE KINGDOM of HEAVEN HAS COME NEAR

JESUS'S MINISTRY IN MATTHEW

8 SIDON

8 TYRE

10 CAESAREA PHILIPPI

MOUNT OF BEATITUDES **4** **6** CAPERNAUM

5 GADARENES

MAGADAN **9**

2 NAZARETH

Sea of Galilee

Mediterranean Sea

Jordan River

ISRAEL

11 JUDEA ACROSS THE JORDAN

JERICHO **12**

JERUSALEM **14** **13** BETHPHAGE

BETHLEHEM **1** **3** JUDEAN WILDERNESS

7 MACHAERUS

Dead Sea

0   40 KM

0   40 MI

N

Sites for 7 and 11 are suggested by scholars, though precise locations are uncertain.

Day 1:
Jesus Is Born

MATTHEW 1

The Genealogy of Jesus Christ

[1] An account of the genealogy of Jesus Christ, the Son of David, the Son of Abraham:

From Abraham to David

[2] Abraham fathered Isaac,
Isaac fathered Jacob,
Jacob fathered Judah and his brothers,
[3] Judah fathered Perez and Zerah by Tamar,
Perez fathered Hezron,
Hezron fathered Aram,
[4] Aram fathered Amminadab,
Amminadab fathered Nahshon,
Nahshon fathered Salmon,
[5] Salmon fathered Boaz by Rahab,
Boaz fathered Obed by Ruth,
Obed fathered Jesse,
[6] and Jesse fathered King David.

From David to the Babylonian Exile

David fathered Solomon by Uriah's wife,
[7] Solomon fathered Rehoboam,
Rehoboam fathered Abijah,
Abijah fathered Asa,
[8] Asa fathered Jehoshaphat,
Jehoshaphat fathered Joram,
Joram fathered Uzziah,
[9] Uzziah fathered Jotham,
Jotham fathered Ahaz,
Ahaz fathered Hezekiah,
[10] Hezekiah fathered Manasseh,
Manasseh fathered Amon,
Amon fathered Josiah,
[11] and Josiah fathered Jeconiah and his brothers
at the time of the exile to Babylon.

From the Exile to the Christ

[12] After the exile to Babylon
Jeconiah fathered Shealtiel,
Shealtiel fathered Zerubbabel,
[13] Zerubbabel fathered Abiud,
Abiud fathered Eliakim,
Eliakim fathered Azor,

continued

JERUSALEM, ISRAEL

[14] Azor fathered Zadok,
Zadok fathered Achim,
Achim fathered Eliud,
[15] Eliud fathered Eleazar,
Eleazar fathered Matthan,
Matthan fathered Jacob,
[16] and Jacob fathered Joseph the husband of Mary,
who gave birth to Jesus who is called the Christ.

[17] So all the generations from Abraham to David were fourteen generations; and from David until the exile to Babylon, fourteen generations; and from the exile to Babylon until the Christ, fourteen generations.

Names in **orange bold** are featured in the "Key People in Matthew" glossary on page 136.

The Nativity of the Christ

[18] The birth of Jesus Christ came about this way: After his mother **Mary** had been engaged to **Joseph**, it was discovered before they came together that she was pregnant from the Holy Spirit. [19] So her husband Joseph, being a righteous man, and not wanting to disgrace her publicly, decided to divorce her secretly.

[20] But after he had considered these things, an angel of the Lord appeared to him in a dream, saying, "Joseph, son of David, don't be afraid to take Mary as your wife, because what has been conceived in her is from the Holy Spirit. [21] She will give birth to a son, and you are to name him Jesus, because he will save his people from their sins."

[22] Now all this took place to fulfill what was spoken by the Lord through the prophet:

[23] See, the virgin will become pregnant
and give birth to a son,
and they will name him Immanuel,

which is translated "God is with us."

[24] When Joseph woke up, he did as the Lord's angel had commanded him. He married her [25] but did not have sexual relations with her until she gave birth to a son. And he named him Jesus.

MATTHEW 2

Wise Men Visit the King

[1] After Jesus was born in **Bethlehem** of Judea in the days of **King Herod**, wise men from the east arrived in Jerusalem, [2] saying, "Where is he who has been born king of the Jews? For we saw his star at its rising and have come to worship him."

[3] When King Herod heard this, he was deeply disturbed, and all Jerusalem with him. [4] So he assembled all the chief priests and scribes of the people and asked them where the Christ would be born.

Locations from the "Jesus's Ministry in Matthew" map on page 12 will be called out in the text as you read.

BETHLEHEM

[5] "In Bethlehem of Judea," they told him, "because this is what was written by the prophet:

> [6] And you, Bethlehem, in the land of Judah,
> are by no means least among the rulers of Judah:
> Because out of you will come a ruler
> who will shepherd my people Israel."

[7] Then Herod secretly summoned the wise men and asked them the exact time the star appeared. [8] He sent them to Bethlehem and said, "Go and search carefully for the child. When you find him, report back to me so that I too can go and worship him."

[9] After hearing the king, they went on their way. And there it was—the star they had seen at its rising. It led them until it came and stopped above the place where the child was. [10] When they saw the star, they were overwhelmed with joy. [11] Entering the house, they saw the child with Mary his mother, and falling to their knees, they worshiped him. Then they opened their treasures and presented him with gifts: gold, frankincense, and myrrh. [12] And being warned in a dream not to go back to Herod, they returned to their own country by another route.

The Flight into Egypt

[13] After they were gone, an angel of the Lord appeared to Joseph in a dream, saying, "Get up! Take the child and his mother, flee to Egypt, and stay there until I tell you. For Herod is about to search for the child to kill him." [14] So he got up, took the child and his mother during the night, and escaped to Egypt. [15] He stayed there until Herod's death, so that what was spoken by the Lord through the prophet might be fulfilled: Out of Egypt I called my Son.

The Massacre of the Innocents

[16] Then Herod, when he realized that he had been outwitted by the wise men, flew into a rage. He gave orders to massacre all the boys in and around Bethlehem who were two years old and under, in keeping with the time he had learned from the wise men. [17] Then what was spoken through Jeremiah the prophet was fulfilled:

> [18] A voice was heard in Ramah,
> weeping, and great mourning,
> Rachel weeping for her children;
> and she refused to be consoled,
> because they are no more.

The Return to Nazareth

[19] After Herod died, an angel of the Lord appeared in a dream to Joseph in Egypt, [20] saying, "Get up, take the child and his mother, and go to the land of Israel, because those who intended to kill the child are dead." [21] So he got up, took the child and his mother, and entered the land of Israel. [22] But when he heard that Archelaus was ruling over Judea in place of his father Herod, he was afraid to go there. And being warned in a dream, he withdrew to the region of Galilee. [23] Then he went and settled in a town called **Nazareth** to fulfill what was spoken through the prophets, that he would be called a Nazarene.

NAZARETH

[2] The people walking in darkness
have seen a great light;
a light has dawned
on those living in the land of darkness.
[3] You have enlarged the nation
and increased its joy.
The people have rejoiced before you
as they rejoice at harvest time
and as they rejoice when dividing spoils.
[4] For you have shattered their oppressive yoke
and the rod on their shoulders,
the staff of their oppressor,
just as you did on the day of Midian.
[5] For every trampling boot of battle
and the bloodied garments of war
will be burned as fuel for the fire.
[6] For a child will be born for us,
a son will be given to us,
and the government will be on his shoulders.
He will be named
Wonderful Counselor, Mighty God,
Eternal Father, Prince of Peace.
[7] The dominion will be vast,
and its prosperity will never end.
He will reign on the throne of David
and over his kingdom,
to establish and sustain it
with justice and righteousness from now on and forever.
The zeal of the LORD of Armies will accomplish this.

ISAIAH 11:1-9

Reign of the Davidic King
[1] Then a shoot will grow from the stump of Jesse,
and a branch from his roots will bear fruit.
[2] The Spirit of the LORD will rest on him—
a Spirit of wisdom and understanding,
a Spirit of counsel and strength,
a Spirit of knowledge and of the fear of the LORD.
[3] His delight will be in the fear of the LORD.
He will not judge
by what he sees with his eyes,

he will not execute justice
by what he hears with his ears,
[4] but he will judge the poor righteously
and execute justice for the oppressed of the land.
He will strike the land
with a scepter from his mouth,
and he will kill the wicked
with a command from his lips.
[5] Righteousness will be a belt around his hips;
faithfulness will be a belt around his waist.

[6] The wolf will dwell with the lamb,
and the leopard will lie down with the goat.
The calf, the young lion, and the fattened calf will be together,
and a child will lead them.
[7] The cow and the bear will graze,
their young ones will lie down together,
and the lion will eat straw like cattle.
[8] An infant will play beside the cobra's pit,
and a toddler will put his hand into a snake's den.
[9] They will not harm or destroy each other
on my entire holy mountain,
for the land will be as full
of the knowledge of the LORD
as the sea is filled with water.

JEREMIAH 31:15

Lament Turned to Joy
This is what the LORD says:

A voice was heard in Ramah,
a lament with bitter weeping—
Rachel weeping for her children,
refusing to be comforted for her children
because they are no more.

OBSERVE   *What is happening in the text?*

REFLECT   *What does it teach me about Jesus?*

APPLY   *What is my response?*

Day 2: Jesus's Ministry Begins

MATTHEW 3

The Herald of the Christ

[1] In those days John the Baptist came, preaching in the wilderness of Judea [2] and saying, "Repent, because the kingdom of heaven has come near!" [3] For he is the one spoken of through the prophet Isaiah, who said:

A voice of one crying out in the wilderness:
Prepare the way for the Lord;
make his paths straight!

[4] Now John had a camel-hair garment with a leather belt around his waist, and his food was locusts and wild honey. [5] Then people from Jerusalem, all Judea, and all the vicinity of the Jordan were going out to him, [6] and they were baptized by him in the Jordan River, confessing their sins.

[7] When he saw many of the **Pharisees** and Sadducees coming to his baptism, he said to them, "Brood of vipers! Who warned you to flee from the coming wrath? [8] Therefore produce fruit consistent with repentance. [9] And don't presume to say to yourselves, 'We have Abraham as our father.' For I tell you that God is able to raise up children for Abraham from these stones. [10] The ax is already at the root of the trees. Therefore, every tree that doesn't produce good fruit will be cut down and thrown into the fire.

[11] "I baptize you with water for repentance, but the one who is coming after me is more powerful than I. I am not worthy to remove his sandals. He himself will baptize you with the Holy Spirit and fire. [12] His winnowing shovel is in his hand, and he will clear his threshing floor and gather his wheat into the barn. But the chaff he will burn with fire that never goes out."

PHARISEES

"Set apart ones" focused on the study and interpretation of Scripture

Ruled the local synagogues and had strong influence in the Jewish community

Believed both the written Law of Moses and oral tradition were authoritative

The Baptism of Jesus

[13] Then Jesus came from Galilee to John at the Jordan, to be baptized by him. [14] But John tried to stop him, saying, "I need to be baptized by you, and yet you come to me?"

[15] Jesus answered him, "Allow it for now, because this is the way for us to fulfill all righteousness." Then John allowed him to be baptized.

[16] When Jesus was baptized, he went up immediately from the water. The heavens suddenly opened for him, and he saw the Spirit of God descending like a dove and coming down on him. [17] And a voice from heaven said: "This is my beloved Son, with whom I am well-pleased."

JUDEAN WILDERNESS

MATTHEW 4

The Temptation of Jesus

¹ Then Jesus was led up by the Spirit into the wilderness to be tempted by the devil. ² After he had fasted forty days and forty nights, he was hungry. ³ Then the tempter approached him and said, "If you are the Son of God, tell these stones to become bread."

⁴ He answered, "It is written: Man must not live on bread alone but on every word that comes from the mouth of God."

⁵ Then the devil took him to the holy city, had him stand on the pinnacle of the temple, ⁶ and said to him, "If you are the Son of God, throw yourself down. For it is written:

He will give his angels orders concerning you,
and they will support you with their hands
so that you will not strike
your foot against a stone."

⁷ Jesus told him, "It is also written: Do not test the Lord your God."

⁸ Again, the devil took him to a very high mountain and showed him all the kingdoms of the world and their splendor. ⁹ And he said to him, "I will give you all these things if you will fall down and worship me."

[10] Then Jesus told him, "Go away, Satan! For it is written: Worship the Lord your God, and serve only him."

[11] Then the devil left him, and angels came and began to serve him.

Ministry in Galilee

[12] When he heard that John had been arrested, he withdrew into Galilee. [13] He left Nazareth and went to live in Capernaum by the sea, in the region of Zebulun and Naphtali. [14] This was to fulfill what was spoken through the prophet Isaiah:

> [15] Land of Zebulun and land of Naphtali,
> along the road by the sea, beyond the Jordan,
> Galilee of the Gentiles.
> [16] The people who live in darkness
> have seen a great light,
> and for those living in the land of the shadow of death,
> a light has dawned.

[17] From then on Jesus began to preach, "Repent, because the kingdom of heaven has come near."

The First Disciples

[18] As he was walking along the Sea of Galilee, he saw two brothers, Simon (who is called Peter), and his brother Andrew. They were casting a net into the sea—for they were fishermen. [19] "Follow me," he told them, "and I will make you fish for people." [20] Immediately they left their nets and followed him.

[21] Going on from there, he saw two other brothers, James the son of Zebedee, and his brother John. They were in a boat with Zebedee their father, preparing their nets, and he called them. [22] Immediately they left the boat and their father and followed him.

Teaching, Preaching, and Healing

[23] Now Jesus began to go all over Galilee, teaching in their synagogues, preaching the good news of the kingdom, and healing every disease and sickness among the people. [24] Then the news about him spread throughout Syria. So they brought to him all those who were afflicted, those suffering from various diseases and intense pains, the demon-possessed, the epileptics, and the paralytics. And he healed them. [25] Large crowds followed him from Galilee, the Decapolis, Jerusalem, Judea, and beyond the Jordan.

ISAIAH 40:3

A voice of one crying out:

> Prepare the way of the LORD in the wilderness;
> make a straight highway for our God in the desert.

MALACHI 4:1–6

The Day of the LORD

[1] "For look, the day is coming, burning like a furnace, when all the arrogant and everyone who commits wickedness will become stubble. The coming day will consume them," says the LORD of Armies, "not leaving them root or branches. [2] But for you who fear my name, the sun of righteousness will rise with healing in its wings, and you will go out and playfully jump like calves from the stall. [3] You will trample the wicked, for they will be ashes under the soles of your feet on the day I am preparing," says the LORD of Armies.

A Final Warning

[4] "Remember the instruction of Moses my servant, the statutes and ordinances I commanded him at Horeb for all Israel. [5] Look, I am going to send you the prophet Elijah before the great and terrible day of the LORD comes. [6] And he will turn the hearts of fathers to their children and the hearts of children to their fathers. Otherwise, I will come and strike the land with a curse."

"Repent, because the kingdom of heaven has come near." 4:17

OBSERVE   *What is happening in the text?*

REFLECT   *What does it teach me about Jesus?*

APPLY   *What is my response?*

12

DISCIPLES

During Jesus's earthly ministry, He chose twelve men to be His disciples. These men followed Jesus, learned His teachings, tended to the needs of His ongoing ministry, and, with the exception of Judas Iscariot, took the lead in carrying out the Great Commission.

Peter, James, and John were particularly close to Jesus (Mk 5:37). These three were present during Jesus's transfiguration (Mk 9:2–8), and they were the only disciples whom Jesus asked to stay near as he prayed in the garden of Gethsemane the night He was betrayed (Mt 26:36–46).

1

Peter

also known as CEPHAS • SIMON, SON OF JONAH • SIMON PETER • SIMON

FAMILY
SON OF JONAH (MT 16:17)
ANDREW'S BROTHER (MT 4:18)

OCCUPATION: FISHERMAN BY TRADE, CALLED TO BE A FISHER OF MEN (MT 4:19)

- Lived in Capernaum and was married (Mt 8:5–14)
- Said Jesus was the Christ, the Son of God (Mt 16:16–19)
- Refused to accept that Jesus had to go to the cross (Mt 16:23)
- Sent with John to secure the Upper Room for the Last Supper (Lk 22:8)
- Denied knowing Jesus when Jesus was on trial (Lk 22:31–34)
- Reinstated by Jesus after the resurrection (Jn 21:15–19)
- Author of 1 and 2 Peter

2

James

also known as BOANERGES, "SON OF THUNDER" • JAMES, SON OF ZEBEDEE
JAMES THE ELDER† • JAMES THE GREAT†

FAMILY
SON OF ZEBEDEE AND SALOME (MT 4:21; 27:56)
JOHN'S BROTHER (MT 4:21)

OCCUPATION: FISHERMAN BY TRADE, WITH HIS FATHER AND BROTHER (MT 4:18-22)

- Sometimes self-centered and conceited (Mk 10:35–37)
- First apostle to be martyred (Ac 12:2)

3

John

also known as BOANERGES, "SON OF THUNDER" • JOHN, SON OF ZEBEDEE
THE DISCIPLE JESUS LOVED • THE EVANGELIST† • THE REVELATOR†

FAMILY
SON OF ZEBEDEE AND SALOME (MT 4:21; 27:56)
JAMES'S BROTHER (MT 4:21)

OCCUPATION: FISHERMAN BY TRADE, WITH HIS FATHER AND BROTHER (MT 4:18-22)

- Sometimes judgmental and self-righteous (Mk 9:38; 10:35–37)
- Exiled to Patmos, where he received his revelation (Rv 1:1, 9)
- Wrote the Gospel bearing his name, along with 1, 2, and 3 John and Revelation.

†Names given outside of the biblical text

Along with Peter, James, and John, these nine disciples were sent out by Jesus to preach about the kingdom of heaven and heal the sick (Mt 10:5–8). All twelve disciples were present at the Last Supper (Mt 26:20).

4

Andrew

also known as PROTOKLETOS, "THE FIRST CALLED"[1]

- First disciple to follow Jesus (Jn 1:35–40)
- Simon Peter's brother (Mt 4:18)
- Fisherman by trade, called to be a fisher of men (Mt 4:19)
- Former disciple of John the Baptist (Jn 1:35–40)
- Told Jesus about the boy with the loaves and fish (Jn 6:8–9)

5

Bartholomew

also known as NATHANAEL

- Educated skeptic (Jn 1:46–47)
- Confessed that Jesus was the Son of God and King of Israel (Jn 1:49)
- Told by Jesus that he would see heaven open and the angels descend on the Son of God (Jn 1:50–51)

6

James

also known as JAMES, SON OF ALPHAEUS • JAMES THE YOUNGER JAMES THE LESS[1]

- Possibly Matthew's brother (Mk 3:18)

7

Matthew

also known as MATTHEW THE TAX COLLECTOR • LEVI, SON OF ALPHAEUS

- Tax collector from Capernaum (Mk 2:1-17)
- Possibly James the Younger's brother (Mk 3:18)
- Called to follow Jesus while working at his tax collector booth (Mt 9:9)
- Humble and repentant (Mt 9:9; 10:2)
- Invited Jesus to dine at his home (Mt 9:10)
- Wrote the Gospel bearing his name

8

Philip

- Third disciple to follow Jesus (Jn 1:43)
- Brought his brother Bartholomew to meet Jesus (Jn 1:45–46)
- Analytical and pragmatic (Jn 6:7)
- Told Jesus about Greeks who wanted to meet with Him (Jn 12:20–22)
- Asked Jesus to help him see the Father (Jn 14:8–9)

9

Simon
also known as SIMON THE ZEALOT • SIMON OF CANAAN

- Part of a political faction committed to opposing Roman rule (Mt 10:4)

10

Thaddaeus
also known as JUDE • JUDAS, SON OF JAMES • LEBBAEUS

- Asked how Jesus would reveal Himself to His disciples in the future (Jn 14:22)

11

Thomas
also known as DIDYMUS, THE TWIN • JUDAS THOMAS • DOUBTING THOMAS[†]

- Probably a twin (Jn 20:24)
- Willing to die for Jesus (Jn 11:16)
- Asked Jesus how to follow Him into the life to come (Jn 14:5)
- Doubted that Jesus had risen from the grave (Jn 20:25)
- Believed in the resurrection after seeing and touching the risen Jesus (Jn 20:28)

12

All but Judas Iscariot were present at the Great Commission (Mt 28:16–20), witnessed Jesus' ascension into heaven (Ac 1:8–9), and were involved in the events surrounding the Holy Spirit's coming at Pentecost (Ac 1–2).

Judas Iscariot
also known as JUDAS THE BETRAYER[†] • JUDAS, SON OF SIMON

- Treasurer for Jesus and the other disciples (Jn 12:5–6)
- Greedy and deceitful (Mt 26:14–16, 25)
- Criticized Mary for "wasting" valuable perfume on Jesus (Jn 12:4–8)
- Left the Upper Room to betray Jesus (Jn 13:2; 21–30)
- Betrayed Jesus for thirty pieces of silver (Mt 26:14–16)
- Remorseful for his betrayal, he chose to end his own life (Mt 27:3–5)
- Replaced by Matthias after the resurrection (Ac 1:26)

[†]*Names given outside of the biblical text*

Day 3:
Jesus Preaches
the Sermon on
the Mount,
Part 1

The Sermon on the Mount

¹ When he saw the crowds, he went up on the **mountain**, and after he sat down, his disciples came to him. ² Then he began to teach them, saying:

The Beatitudes

³ "Blessed are the poor in spirit,
for the kingdom of heaven is theirs.
⁴ Blessed are those who mourn,
for they will be comforted.
⁵ Blessed are the humble,
for they will inherit the earth.
⁶ Blessed are those who hunger and thirst for righteousness,
for they will be filled.
⁷ Blessed are the merciful,
for they will be shown mercy.
⁸ Blessed are the pure in heart,
for they will see God.
⁹ Blessed are the peacemakers,
for they will be called sons of God.
¹⁰ Blessed are those who are persecuted because of righteousness,
for the kingdom of heaven is theirs.

¹¹ "You are blessed when they insult you and persecute you and falsely say every kind of evil against you because of me. ¹² Be glad and rejoice, because your reward is great in heaven. For that is how they persecuted the prophets who were before you.

Believers Are Salt and Light

¹³ "You are the salt of the earth. But if the salt should lose its taste, how can it be made salty? It's no longer good for anything but to be thrown out and trampled under people's feet.

¹⁴ "You are the light of the world. A city situated on a hill cannot be hidden. ¹⁵ No one lights a lamp and puts it under a basket, but rather on a lampstand, and it gives light for all who are in the house. ¹⁶ In the same way, let your light shine before others, so that they may see your good works and give glory to your Father in heaven.

Christ Fulfills the Law

¹⁷ "Don't think that I came to abolish the Law or the Prophets. I did not come to abolish but to fulfill. ¹⁸ For truly I tell you, until heaven and earth pass away, not the smallest letter or one stroke of a letter will pass away from the law until all things are accomplished. ¹⁹ Therefore, whoever breaks one of the least of these commands and teaches others to do the same will be called least in the kingdom of

MOUNT OF
BEATITUDES

"I did not come to abolish but to fulfill."

5:17

heaven. But whoever does and teaches these commands will be called great in the kingdom of heaven. ²⁰ For I tell you, unless your righteousness surpasses that of the scribes and Pharisees, you will never get into the kingdom of heaven.

Murder Begins in the Heart

²¹ "You have heard that it was said to our ancestors, Do not murder, and whoever murders will be subject to judgment. ²² But I tell you, everyone who is angry with his brother or sister will be subject to judgment. Whoever insults his brother or sister, will be subject to the court. Whoever says, 'You fool!' will be subject to hellfire. ²³ So if you are offering your gift on the altar, and there you remember that your brother or sister has something against you, ²⁴ leave your gift there in front of the altar. First go and be reconciled with your brother or sister, and then come and offer your gift. ²⁵ Reach a settlement quickly with your adversary while you're on the way with him to the court, or your adversary will hand you over to the judge, and the judge to the officer, and you will be thrown into prison. ²⁶ Truly I tell you, you will never get out of there until you have paid the last penny.

Adultery Begins in the Heart

²⁷ "You have heard that it was said, Do not commit adultery. ²⁸ But I tell you, everyone who looks at a woman lustfully has already committed adultery with her in his heart. ²⁹ If your right eye causes you to sin, gouge it out and throw it away. For it is better that you lose one of the parts of your body than for your whole body to be thrown into hell. ³⁰ And if your right hand causes you to sin, cut it off and throw it away. For it is better that you lose one of the parts of your body than for your whole body to go into hell.

Divorce Practices Censured

³¹ "It was also said, Whoever divorces his wife must give her a written notice of divorce. ³² But I tell you, everyone who divorces his wife, except in a case of sexual immorality, causes her to commit adultery. And whoever marries a divorced woman commits adultery.

Tell the Truth

³³ "Again, you have heard that it was said to our ancestors, You must not break your oath, but you must keep your oaths to the Lord. ³⁴ But I tell you, don't take an oath at all: either by heaven, because it is God's throne; ³⁵ or by the earth, because it is his footstool; or by Jerusalem, because it is the city of the great King. ³⁶ Do not swear by your head, because you cannot make a single hair white or black. ³⁷ But let your 'yes' mean 'yes,' and your 'no' mean 'no.' Anything more than this is from the evil one.

Go the Second Mile

³⁸ "You have heard that it was said, An eye for an eye and a tooth for a tooth. ³⁹ But I tell you, don't resist an evildoer. On the contrary, if anyone slaps you on your right cheek, turn the other to him also. ⁴⁰ As for the one who wants to sue you and take away your shirt, let him have your coat as well. ⁴¹ And if anyone forces you to go one mile, go with him two. ⁴² Give to the one who asks you, and don't turn away from the one who wants to borrow from you.

Love Your Enemies

[43] "You have heard that it was said, Love your neighbor and hate your enemy. [44] But I tell you, love your enemies and pray for those who persecute you, [45] so that you may be children of your Father in heaven. For he causes his sun to rise on the evil and the good, and sends rain on the righteous and the unrighteous. [46] For if you love those who love you, what reward will you have? Don't even the tax collectors do the same? [47] And if you greet only your brothers and sisters, what are you doing out of the ordinary? Don't even the Gentiles do the same? [48] Be perfect, therefore, as your heavenly Father is perfect."

ROMANS 12:9-21

Christian Ethics

[9] Let love be without hypocrisy. Detest evil; cling to what is good. [10] Love one another deeply as brothers and sisters. Outdo one another in showing honor. [11] Do not lack diligence in zeal; be fervent in the Spirit; serve the Lord. [12] Rejoice in hope; be patient in affliction; be persistent in prayer. [13] Share with the saints in their needs; pursue hospitality. [14] Bless those who persecute you; bless and do not curse. [15] Rejoice with those who rejoice; weep with those who weep. [16] Live in harmony with one another. Do not be proud; instead, associate with the humble. Do not be wise in your own estimation. [17] Do not repay anyone evil for evil. Give careful thought to do what is honorable in everyone's eyes. [18] If possible, as far as it depends on you, live at peace with everyone. [19] Friends, do not avenge yourselves; instead, leave room for God's wrath, because it is written, Vengeance belongs to me; I will repay, says the Lord. [20] But

> If your enemy is hungry, feed him.
> If he is thirsty, give him something to drink.
> For in so doing
> you will be heaping fiery coals on his head.

[21] Do not be conquered by evil, but conquer evil with good.

2 TIMOTHY 3:16-17

[16] All Scripture is inspired by God and is profitable for teaching, for rebuking, for correcting, for training in righteousness, [17] so that the man of God may be complete, equipped for every good work.

OBSERVE   *What is happening in the text?*

REFLECT   *What does it teach me about Jesus?*

APPLY   *What is my response?*

Day 4: Jesus Preaches the Sermon on the Mount, Part 2

MATTHEW 6

How to Give

[1] "Be careful not to practice your righteousness in front of others to be seen by them. Otherwise, you have no reward with your Father in heaven. [2] So whenever you give to the poor, don't sound a trumpet before you, as the hypocrites do in the synagogues and on the streets, to be applauded by people. Truly I tell you, they have their reward. [3] But when you give to the poor, don't let your left hand know what your right hand is doing, [4] so that your giving may be in secret. And your Father who sees in secret will reward you.

How to Pray

[5] "Whenever you pray, you must not be like the hypocrites, because they love to pray standing in the synagogues and on the street corners to be seen by people. Truly I tell you, they have their reward. [6] But when you pray, go into your private room, shut your door, and pray to your Father who is in secret. And your Father who sees in secret will reward you. [7] When you pray, don't babble like the Gentiles, since they imagine they'll be heard for their many words. [8] Don't be like them, because your Father knows the things you need before you ask him.

The Model Prayer

[9] "Therefore, you should pray like this:

Our Father in heaven,
your name be honored as holy.
[10] Your kingdom come.
Your will be done
on earth as it is in heaven.
[11] Give us today our daily bread.
[12] And forgive us our debts,
as we also have forgiven our debtors.
[13] And do not bring us into temptation,
but deliver us from the evil one.

[14] "For if you forgive others their offenses, your heavenly Father will forgive you as well. [15] But if you don't forgive others, your Father will not forgive your offenses.

How to Fast

[16] "Whenever you fast, don't be gloomy like the hypocrites. For they make their faces unattractive so that their fasting is obvious to people. Truly I tell you, they have their reward. [17] But when you fast, put oil on your head and wash your face, [18] so that your fasting isn't obvious to others but to your Father who is in secret. And your Father who sees in secret will reward you.

continued

MOUNT OF BEATITUDES

God and Possessions

19 "Don't store up for yourselves treasures on earth, where moth and rust destroy and where thieves break in and steal. 20 But store up for yourselves treasures in heaven, where neither moth nor rust destroys, and where thieves don't break in and steal. 21 For where your treasure is, there your heart will be also.

22 "The eye is the lamp of the body. If your eye is healthy, your whole body will be full of light. 23 But if your eye is bad, your whole body will be full of darkness. So if the light within you is darkness, how deep is that darkness!

24 "No one can serve two masters, since either he will hate one and love the other, or he will be devoted to one and despise the other. You cannot serve both God and money.

The Cure for Anxiety

25 "Therefore I tell you: Don't worry about your life, what you will eat or what you will drink; or about your body, what you will wear. Isn't life more than food and the body more than clothing? 26 Consider the birds of the sky: They don't sow or reap or gather into barns, yet your heavenly Father feeds them. Aren't you worth more than they? 27 Can any of you add one moment to his life-span by worrying? 28 And why do you worry about clothes? Observe how the wildflowers of the field grow: They don't labor or spin thread. 29 Yet I tell you that not even Solomon in all his splendor was adorned like one of these. 30 If that's how God clothes the grass of the field, which is here today and thrown into the furnace tomorrow, won't he do much more for you—you of little faith? 31 So don't worry, saying, 'What will we eat?' or 'What will we drink?' or 'What will we wear?' 32 For the **Gentiles** eagerly seek all these things, and your heavenly Father knows that you need them. 33 But seek first the kingdom of God and his righteousness, and all these things will be provided for you. 34 Therefore don't worry about tomorrow, because tomorrow will worry about itself. Each day has enough trouble of its own."

GENTILES

All non-Jewish people and people groups

Were considered ceremonially unclean by Jewish people

Were considered by Jewish people to be outsiders to God's covenant promises

Do Not Judge

1 "Do not judge, so that you won't be judged. 2 For you will be judged by the same standard with which you judge others, and you will be measured by the same measure you use. 3 Why do you look at the splinter in your brother's eye but don't notice the beam of wood in your own eye? 4 Or how can you say to your brother, 'Let me take the splinter out of your eye,' and look, there's a beam of wood in your own eye? 5 Hypocrite! First take the beam of wood out of your eye, and then you will see clearly to take the splinter out of your brother's eye. 6 Don't give what is holy to dogs or toss your pearls before pigs, or they will trample them under their feet, turn, and tear you to pieces.

Ask, Search, Knock

7 "Ask, and it will be given to you. Seek, and you will find. Knock, and the door will be opened to you. 8 For everyone who asks receives, and the one who seeks finds, and to the one who knocks, the door will be opened. 9 Who among you, if his son asks him for bread, will give him a stone? 10 Or if he asks for a fish, will give him a snake? 11 If you then, who are evil, know how to give good gifts to your children, how much more will your Father in heaven give good things to those who ask him. 12 Therefore, whatever you want others to do for you, do also the same for them, for this is the Law and the Prophets.

Entering the Kingdom

13 "Enter through the narrow gate. For the gate is wide and the road broad that leads to destruction, and there are many who go through it. 14 How narrow is the gate and difficult the road that leads to life, and few find it.

15 "Be on your guard against false prophets who come to you in sheep's clothing but inwardly are ravaging wolves. 16 You'll recognize them by their fruit. Are grapes gathered from thornbushes or figs from thistles? 17 In the same way, every good tree produces good fruit, but a bad tree produces bad fruit. 18 A good tree can't produce bad fruit; neither can a bad tree produce good fruit. 19 Every tree that doesn't produce good fruit is cut down and thrown into the fire. 20 So you'll recognize them by their fruit.

21 "Not everyone who says to me, 'Lord, Lord,' will enter the kingdom of heaven, but only the one who does the will of my Father in heaven. 22 On that day many will say to me, 'Lord, Lord, didn't we prophesy in your name, drive out demons in your name, and do many miracles in your name?' 23 Then I will announce to them, 'I never knew you. Depart from me, you lawbreakers!'

The Two Foundations
24 "Therefore, everyone who hears these words of mine and acts on them will be like a wise man who built his house on the rock. 25 The rain fell, the rivers rose, and the winds blew and pounded that house. Yet it didn't collapse, because its foundation was on the rock. 26 But everyone who hears these words of mine and doesn't act on them will be like a foolish man who built his house on the sand. 27 The rain fell, the rivers rose, the winds blew and pounded that house, and it collapsed. It collapsed with a great crash."

28 When Jesus had finished saying these things, the crowds were astonished at his teaching, 29 because he was teaching them like one who had authority, and not like their scribes.

1 CHRONICLES 29:11-13

11 Yours, LORD, is the greatness and the power and the glory and the splendor and the majesty, for everything in the heavens and on earth belongs to you. Yours, LORD, is the kingdom, and you are exalted as head over all. 12 Riches and honor come from you, and you are the ruler of everything. Power and might are in your hand, and it is in your hand to make great and to give strength to all. 13 Now therefore, our God, we give you thanks and praise your glorious name.

1 JOHN 2:28-29

God's Children
28 So now, little children, remain in him so that when he appears we may have confidence and not be ashamed before him at his coming. 29 If you know that he is righteous, you know this as well: Everyone who does what is right has been born of him.

OBSERVE   *What is happening in the text?*

REFLECT   *What does it teach me about Jesus?*

APPLY   *What is my response?*

Day 5:
Jesus Heals

A Man Cleansed

[1] When he came down from the mountain, large crowds followed him. [2] Right away a man with leprosy came up and knelt before him, saying, "Lord, if you are willing, you can make me clean."

[3] Reaching out his hand, Jesus touched him, saying, "I am willing; be made clean." Immediately his leprosy was cleansed. [4] Then Jesus told him, "See that you don't tell anyone; but go, show yourself to the priest, and offer the gift that Moses commanded, as a testimony to them."

A Centurion's Faith

[5] When he entered Capernaum, a **centurion** came to him, pleading with him, [6] "Lord, my servant is lying at home paralyzed, in terrible agony."

[7] He said to him, "Am I to come and heal him?"

[8] "Lord," the centurion replied, "I am not worthy to have you come under my roof. But just say the word, and my servant will be healed. [9] For I too am a man under authority, having soldiers under my command. I say to this one, 'Go,' and he goes; and to another, 'Come,' and he comes; and to my servant, 'Do this!' and he does it."

CENTURIONS

Professional commanding officers in the Roman army

Commanded roughly one hundred soldiers

Had military experience, formal education, and respect in the public eye

[10] Hearing this, Jesus was amazed and said to those following him, "Truly I tell you, I have not found anyone in Israel with so great a faith. [11] I tell you that many will come from east and west to share the banquet with Abraham, Isaac, and Jacob in the kingdom of heaven. [12] But the sons of the kingdom will be thrown into the outer darkness where there will be weeping and gnashing of teeth." [13] Then Jesus told the centurion, "Go. As you have believed, let it be done for you." And his servant was healed that very moment.

Healings at Capernaum

[14] Jesus went into Peter's house and saw his mother-in-law lying in bed with a fever. [15] So he touched her hand, and the fever left her. Then she got up and began to serve him. [16] When evening came, they brought to him many who were demon-possessed. He drove out the spirits with a word and healed all who were sick, [17] so that what was spoken through the prophet Isaiah might be fulfilled:

He himself took our weaknesses
and carried our diseases.

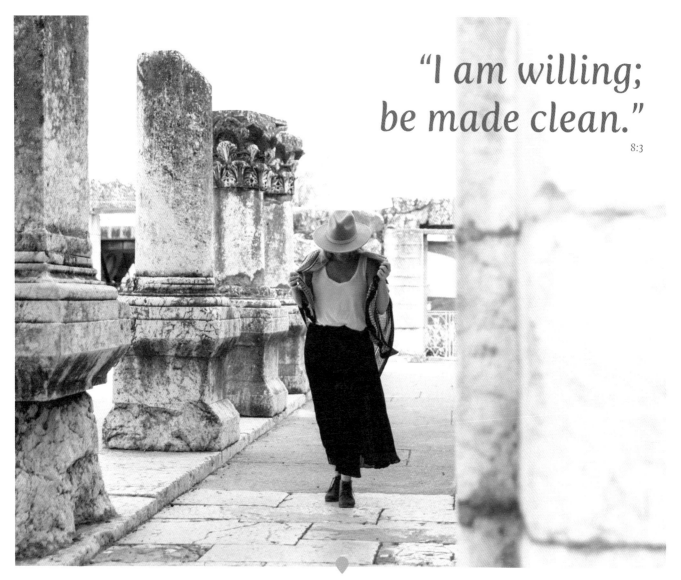

> # "I am willing; be made clean."
> 8:3

The Cost of Following Jesus

¹⁸ When Jesus saw a large crowd around him, he gave the order to go to the other side of the sea. ¹⁹ A scribe approached him and said, "Teacher, I will follow you wherever you go."

²⁰ Jesus told him, "Foxes have dens, and birds of the sky have nests, but the Son of Man has no place to lay his head."

²¹ "Lord," another of his disciples said, "first let me go bury my father."

²² But Jesus told him, "Follow me, and let the dead bury their own dead."

Wind and Wave Obey Jesus

²³ As he got into the boat, his disciples followed him. ²⁴ Suddenly, a violent storm arose on the sea, so that the boat was being swamped by the waves—but Jesus kept sleeping. ²⁵ So the disciples came and woke him up, saying, "Lord, save us! We're going to die!"

²⁶ He said to them, "Why are you afraid, you of little faith?" Then he got up and rebuked the winds and the sea, and there was a great calm.

²⁷ The men were amazed and asked, "What kind of man is this? Even the winds and the sea obey him!"

GADARENES

Demons Driven Out by Jesus

²⁸ When he had come to the other side, to the region of the **Gadarenes**, two demon-possessed men met him as they came out of the tombs. They were so violent that no one could pass that way. ²⁹ Suddenly they shouted, "What do you have to do with us, Son of God? Have you come here to torment us before the time?"

³⁰ A long way off from them, a large herd of pigs was feeding. ³¹ "If you drive us out," the demons begged him, "send us into the herd of pigs."

³² "Go!" he told them. So when they had come out, they entered the pigs, and the whole herd rushed down the steep bank into the sea and perished in the water. ³³ Then the men who tended them fled. They went into the city and reported everything, especially what had happened to those who were demon-possessed. ³⁴ At that, the whole town went out to meet Jesus. When they saw him, they begged him to leave their region.

2 SAMUEL 22:16

The depths of the sea became visible,
the foundations of the world were exposed
at the rebuke of the LORD,
at the blast of the breath of his nostrils.

ISAIAH 53:4–5

⁴ Yet he himself bore our sicknesses,
and he carried our pains;
but we in turn regarded him stricken,
struck down by God, and afflicted.
⁵ But he was pierced because of our rebellion,
crushed because of our iniquities;
punishment for our peace was on him,
and we are healed by his wounds.

OBSERVE   *What is happening in the text?*

REFLECT   *What does it teach me about Jesus?*

APPLY   *What is my response?*

Day 6:
Grace Day

Use this day to pray, rest, and reflect
on this week's reading, giving thanks
for the grace that is ours in Christ.

1 Chronicles 29:11

YOURS, LORD, IS THE GREATNESS AND
THE POWER AND THE GLORY AND THE
SPLENDOR AND THE MAJESTY, FOR
EVERYTHING IN THE HEAVENS AND
ON EARTH BELONGS TO YOU. YOURS,
LORD, IS THE KINGDOM, AND YOU
ARE EXALTED AS HEAD OVER ALL.

Day 7:
Weekly Truth

Scripture is God-breathed and true. When we memorize it, we carry the good news of the gospel of Jesus with us wherever we go.

This week we will memorize the key verse for the Gospel of Matthew.

Matthew 4:17

From then on Jesus began to preach, "Repent, because the kingdom of heaven has come near."

CENTURIONS

Matthew 8:5–13, Matthew 27:54

Professional commanding officers in the Roman army

COMMANDED ROUGHLY ONE HUNDRED SOLDIERS

Had military experience, formal education, and respect in the public eye

ELDERS OF THE PEOPLE

Matthew 12:23–27, Matthew 16:21

A council of men from prominent Jewish families

Part of the Sanhedrin

HELD LEADERSHIP ROLE IN THE GOVERNMENT OF THE LOCAL SYNAGOGUE

KEY GROUPS IN MATTHEW

HERODIANS

Matthew 22:15–22

Jews who supported Herod the Great's descendants serving as rulers over the land

Joined with Pharisees in a plot to kill Jesus

TRIED TO TRICK JESUS INTO SAYING PEOPLE SHOULDN'T PAY TAXES

JEWS

Matthew 2:2, Matthew 27:11

From Judea and Galilee

DESCENDANTS OF ABRAHAM

Believers in one God: the God of Abraham, Isaac, and Jacob

MONEY CHANGERS

Matthew 21:12–13

Responsible for exchanging other currencies for Jewish money

Set up tables in the temple so worshipers could get the correct currency to pay the temple tax and buy sacrifices

OFTEN PROFITED GREATLY BY CHARGING INTEREST RATES RANGING FROM 20% TO 300%

GENTILES

Matthew 6:32, Matthew 20:19

Considered ceremonially unclean by Jewish people

ALL NON-JEWISH PEOPLE AND PEOPLE GROUPS

Considered by Jewish people to be outsiders to God's covenant promises

PHARISEES

Matthew 3:7, Matthew 12:1–8

"Set apart ones" focused on the study and interpretation of the Law of Moses

RULED THE LOCAL SYNAGOGUES AND HAD STRONG INFLUENCE IN THE JEWISH COMMUNITY

Believed both the written Law of Moses and oral tradition were authoritative

PRIESTS/CHIEF PRIESTS/ HIGH PRIESTS

Matthew 20:17–18, Matthew 21:14–17

Official worship leaders for the Jewish people

Represented Israel before God and offered sacrifices on behalf of the people

THE MOST POWERFUL JEWS IN JERUSALEM

SADDUCEES

Matthew 16:1–12, Matthew 22:23–33

Politically oriented and focused on maintaining the beliefs and practices of the past

RESPONSIBLE FOR THE TEMPLE AND ITS SERVICES

Did not believe in the resurrection of the dead and denied the existence of demons and angels

THE SANHEDRIN

Matthew 26:57–68

A seventy-one-member Jewish council in Jerusalem, run by the high priest

MADE UP OF SADDUCEES, PHARISEES, PRIESTS, AND ELDERS OF THE PEOPLE

Had local authority over the Jewish community under Roman oversight

SCRIBES

Matthew 12:38–42, Matthew 15:1–9

Largely made up of Pharisees

PROFESSIONAL GROUP TRAINED IN COPYING AND INTERPRETING THE LAW OF MOSES

Led the plan to kill Jesus

TAX COLLECTORS

Matthew 9:9–11

Contracted by the Roman government to collect taxes

Collected additional profit along with the taxes for their pay

REGARDED AS TREASONOUS, GREEDY, AND DISHONEST BY FELLOW JEWS

ZEALOTS

Matthew 10:4

An extreme political sect committed to resisting Rome

Believed only God had the right to rule the Jews and were willing to die for that belief

CONSIDERED THEIR PATRIOTISM AND RELIGIOUS BELIEFS TO BE INSEPARABLE

Day 8:
Jesus Forgives

The Son of Man Forgives and Heals

¹ So he got into a boat, crossed over, and came to **his own town**. ² Just then some men brought to him a paralytic lying on a stretcher. Seeing their faith, Jesus told the paralytic, "Have courage, son, your sins are forgiven."

³ At this, some of the scribes said to themselves, "He's blaspheming!"

⁴ Perceiving their thoughts, Jesus said, "Why are you thinking evil things in your hearts? ⁵ For which is easier: to say, 'Your sins are forgiven,' or to say, 'Get up and walk'? ⁶ But so that you may know that the Son of Man has authority on earth to forgive sins"—then he told the paralytic, "Get up, take your stretcher, and go home." ⁷ So he got up and went home. ⁸ When the crowds saw this, they were awestruck and gave glory to God, who had given such authority to men.

The Call of Matthew

⁹ As Jesus went on from there, he saw a man named Matthew sitting at the toll booth, and he said to him, "Follow me," and he got up and followed him.

¹⁰ While he was reclining at the table in the house, many **tax collectors** and sinners came to eat with Jesus and his disciples. ¹¹ When the Pharisees saw this, they asked his disciples, "Why does your teacher eat with tax collectors and sinners?"

¹² Now when he heard this, he said, "It is not those who are well who need a doctor, but those who are sick. ¹³ Go and learn what this means: I desire mercy and not sacrifice. For I didn't come to call the righteous, but sinners."

TAX COLLECTORS

Contracted by the Roman government to collect taxes

Collected additional profit along with the taxes for their pay

Were regarded as treasonous, greedy, and dishonest by fellow Jews

A Question about Fasting

¹⁴ Then John's disciples came to him, saying, "Why do we and the Pharisees fast often, but your disciples do not fast?"

¹⁵ Jesus said to them, "Can the wedding guests be sad while the groom is with them? The time will come when the groom will be taken away from them, and then they will fast. ¹⁶ No one patches an old garment with unshrunk cloth, because the patch pulls away from the garment and makes the tear worse. ¹⁷ And no one puts new wine into old wineskins. Otherwise, the skins burst, the wine spills out, and the skins are ruined. No, they put new wine into fresh wineskins, and both are preserved."

"Your faith has saved you."

A Girl Restored and a Woman Healed

18 As he was telling them these things, suddenly one of the leaders came and knelt down before him, saying, "My daughter just died, but come and lay your hand on her, and she will live." 19 So Jesus and his disciples got up and followed him.

20 Just then, a woman who had suffered from bleeding for twelve years approached from behind and touched the end of his robe, 21 for she said to herself, "If I can just touch his robe, I'll be made well."

22 Jesus turned and saw her. "Have courage, daughter," he said. "Your faith has saved you." And the woman was made well from that moment.

23 When Jesus came to the leader's house, he saw the flute players and a crowd lamenting loudly. 24 "Leave," he said, "because the girl is not dead but asleep." And they laughed at him. 25 After the crowd had been put outside, he went in and took her by the hand, and the girl got up. 26 Then news of this spread throughout that whole area.

Healing the Blind

27 As Jesus went on from there, two blind men followed him, calling out, "Have mercy on us, Son of David!"

28 When he entered the house, the blind men approached him, and Jesus said to them, "Do you believe that I can do this?"

They said to him, "Yes, Lord."

29 Then he touched their eyes, saying, "Let it be done for you according to your faith." 30 And their eyes were opened. Then Jesus warned them sternly, "Be sure that no one finds out." 31 But they went out and spread the news about him throughout that whole area.

Driving Out a Demon

32 Just as they were going out, a demon-possessed man who was unable to speak was brought to him. 33 When the demon had been driven out, the man who had been mute spoke, and the crowds were amazed, saying, "Nothing like this has ever been seen in Israel!"

34 But the Pharisees said, "He drives out demons by the ruler of the demons."

The Lord of the Harvest

35 Jesus continued going around to all the towns and villages, teaching in their synagogues, preaching the good news of the kingdom, and healing every disease and every sickness. 36 When he saw the crowds, he felt compassion for them, because they were distressed and dejected, like sheep without a shepherd. 37 Then he said to his disciples, "The harvest is abundant, but the workers are few. 38 Therefore, pray to the Lord of the harvest to send out workers into his harvest."

Purification Ritual

[11] The person who touches any human corpse will be unclean for seven days. [12] He is to purify himself with the water on the third day and the seventh day; then he will be clean. But if he does not purify himself on the third and seventh days, he will not be clean. [13] Anyone who touches a body of a person who has died, and does not purify himself, defiles the tabernacle of the LORD. That person will be cut off from Israel. He remains unclean because the water for impurity has not been sprinkled on him, and his uncleanness is still on him.

[14] This is the law when a person dies in a tent: everyone who enters the tent and everyone who is already in the tent will be unclean for seven days, [15] and any open container without a lid tied on it is unclean. [16] Anyone in the open field who touches a person who has been killed by the sword or has died, or who even touches a human bone, or a grave, will be unclean for seven days. [17] For the purification of the unclean person, they are to take some of the ashes of the burnt sin offering, put them in a jar, and add fresh water to them. [18] A person who is clean is to take hyssop, dip it in the water, and sprinkle the tent, all the furnishings, and the people who were there. He is also to sprinkle the one who touched a bone, a grave, a corpse, or a person who had been killed.

[19] The one who is clean is to sprinkle the unclean person on the third day and the seventh day. After he purifies the unclean person on the seventh day, the one being purified must wash his clothes and bathe in water, and he will be clean by evening. [20] But a person who is unclean and does not purify himself, that person will be cut off from the assembly because he has defiled the sanctuary of the LORD. The water for impurity has not been sprinkled on him; he is unclean. [21] This is a permanent statute for them. The person who sprinkles the water for impurity is to wash his clothes, and whoever touches the water for impurity will be unclean until evening.

[19] I will take you to be my wife forever.
I will take you to be my wife in righteousness,
justice, love, and compassion.
[20] I will take you to be my wife in faithfulness,
and you will know the LORD.

OBSERVE   *What is happening in the text?*

REFLECT   *What does it teach me about Jesus?*

APPLY   *What is my response?*

Week Two

MATTHEW 10

Commissioning the Twelve

[1] Summoning his twelve disciples, he gave them authority over unclean spirits, to drive them out and to heal every disease and sickness. [2] These are the names of the twelve apostles: First, Simon, who is called Peter, and Andrew his brother; James the son of Zebedee, and John his brother; [3] Philip and Bartholomew; Thomas and Matthew the tax collector; James the son of Alphaeus, and Thaddaeus; [4] Simon the **Zealot**, and Judas Iscariot, who also betrayed him.

[5] Jesus sent out these twelve after giving them instructions: "Don't take the road that leads to the Gentiles, and don't enter any Samaritan town. [6] Instead, go to the lost sheep of the house of Israel. [7] As you go, proclaim: 'The kingdom of heaven has come near.' [8] Heal the sick, raise the dead, cleanse those with leprosy, drive out demons. Freely you received, freely give. [9] Don't acquire gold, silver, or copper for your money-belts. [10] Don't take a traveling bag for the road, or an extra shirt, sandals, or a staff, for the worker is worthy of his food. [11] When you enter any town or village, find out who is worthy, and stay there until you leave. [12] Greet a household when you enter it, [13] and if the household is worthy, let your peace be on it; but if it is unworthy, let your peace return to you. [14] If anyone does not welcome you or listen to your words, shake the dust off your feet when you leave that house or town. [15] Truly I tell you, it will be more tolerable on the day of judgment for the land of Sodom and Gomorrah than for that town.

ZEALOTS

An extreme political sect committed to resisting Rome

Believed only God had the right to rule the Jews and were willing to die for that belief

Considered their patriotism and religious beliefs to be inseparable

Persecutions Predicted

[16] "Look, I'm sending you out like sheep among wolves. Therefore be as shrewd as serpents and as innocent as doves. [17] Beware of them, because they will hand you over to local courts and flog you in their synagogues. [18] You will even be brought before governors and kings because of me, to bear witness to them and to the Gentiles. [19] But when they hand you over, don't worry about how or what you are to speak. For you will be given what to say at that hour, [20] because it isn't you speaking, but the Spirit of your Father is speaking through you.

[21] "Brother will betray brother to death, and a father his child. Children will rise up against parents and have them put to death. [22] You will be hated by everyone because of my name. But the one who endures to the end will be saved. [23] When they persecute you in one town, flee to another. For truly I tell you, you will not have gone through the towns of Israel before the Son of Man comes. [24] A disciple is not above his teacher, or a slave above his master. [25] It is enough for a disciple to become like his teacher and a slave like his master. If they called the head of the house 'Beelzebul,' how much more the members of his household!

Fear God

²⁶ "Therefore, don't be afraid of them, since there is nothing covered that won't be uncovered and nothing hidden that won't be made known. ²⁷ What I tell you in the dark, speak in the light. What you hear in a whisper, proclaim on the housetops. ²⁸ Don't fear those who kill the body but are not able to kill the soul; rather, fear him who is able to destroy both soul and body in hell. ²⁹ Aren't two sparrows sold for a penny? Yet not one of them falls to the ground without your Father's consent. ³⁰ But even the hairs of your head have all been counted. ³¹ So don't be afraid; you are worth more than many sparrows.

> ## "You are worth more than many sparrows."
>
> 10:31

Acknowledging Christ

[32] "Therefore, everyone who will acknowledge me before others, I will also acknowledge him before my Father in heaven. [33] But whoever denies me before others, I will also deny him before my Father in heaven. [34] Don't assume that I came to bring peace on the earth. I did not come to bring peace, but a sword. [35] For I came to turn

a man against his father,
a daughter against her mother,
a daughter-in-law against her mother-in-law;
[36] and a man's enemies will be
the members of his household.

[37] The one who loves a father or mother more than me is not worthy of me; the one who loves a son or daughter more than me is not worthy of me. [38] And whoever doesn't take up his cross and follow me is not worthy of me. [39] Anyone who finds his life will lose it, and anyone who loses his life because of me will find it.

A Cup of Cold Water

[40] "The one who welcomes you welcomes me, and the one who welcomes me welcomes him who sent me. [41] Anyone who welcomes a prophet because he is a prophet will receive a prophet's reward. And anyone who welcomes a righteous person because he's righteous will receive a righteous person's reward. [42] And whoever gives even a cup of cold water to one of these little ones because he is a disciple, truly I tell you, he will never lose his reward."

ACTS 1:13

When they arrived, they went to the room upstairs where they were staying: Peter, John, James, Andrew, Philip, Thomas, Bartholomew, Matthew, James the son of Alphaeus, Simon the Zealot, and Judas the son of James.

JAMES 2:1-7

The Sin of Favoritism

[1] My brothers and sisters, do not show favoritism as you hold on to the faith in our glorious Lord Jesus Christ. [2] For if someone comes into your meeting wearing a gold ring and dressed in fine clothes, and a poor person dressed in filthy clothes also comes in, [3] if you look with favor on the one wearing the fine clothes and say, "Sit here in a good place," and yet you say to the poor person, "Stand over there," or "Sit here on the floor by my footstool," [4] haven't you made distinctions among yourselves and become judges with evil thoughts?

[5] Listen, my dear brothers and sisters: Didn't God choose the poor in this world to be rich in faith and heirs of the kingdom that he has promised to those who love him? [6] Yet you have dishonored the poor. Don't the rich oppress you and drag you into court? [7] Don't they blaspheme the good name that was invoked over you?

OBSERVE   *What is happening in the text?*

REFLECT   *What does it teach me about Jesus?*

APPLY   *What is my response?*

Day 10: Jesus Gives Rest

John the Baptist Doubts

¹ When Jesus had finished giving instructions to his twelve disciples, he moved on from there to teach and preach in their towns. ² Now when John heard in prison what the Christ was doing, he sent a message through his disciples ³ and asked him, "Are you the one who is to come, or should we expect someone else?"

⁴ Jesus replied to them, "Go and report to John what you hear and see: ⁵ The blind receive their sight, the lame walk, those with leprosy are cleansed, the deaf hear, the dead are raised, and the poor are told the good news, ⁶ and blessed is the one who isn't offended by me."

⁷ As these men were leaving, Jesus began to speak to the crowds about John: "What did you go out into the wilderness to see? A reed swaying in the wind? ⁸ What then did you go out to see? A man dressed in soft clothes? See, those who wear soft clothes are in royal palaces. ⁹ What then did you go out to see? A prophet? Yes, I tell you, and more than a prophet. ¹⁰ This is the one about whom it is written:

> See, I am sending my messenger ahead of you;
> he will prepare your way before you.

¹¹ "Truly I tell you, among those born of women no one greater than John the Baptist has appeared, but the least in the kingdom of heaven is greater than he. ¹² From the days of John the Baptist until now, the kingdom of heaven has been suffering violence, and the violent have been seizing it by force. ¹³ For all the prophets and the law prophesied until John. ¹⁴ And if you're willing to accept it, he is the Elijah who is to come. ¹⁵ Let anyone who has ears listen.

An Unresponsive Generation

¹⁶ "To what should I compare this generation? It's like children sitting in the marketplaces who call out to other children:

> ¹⁷ We played the flute for you,
> but you didn't dance;
> we sang a lament,
> but you didn't mourn!

¹⁸ For John came neither eating nor drinking, and they say, 'He has a demon!' ¹⁹ The Son of Man came eating and drinking, and they say, 'Look, a glutton and a drunkard, a friend of tax collectors and sinners!' Yet wisdom is vindicated by her deeds."

continued

Week Two

JAFFA PORT

"For my yoke is easy and my burden is light."

11:30

[20] Then he proceeded to denounce the towns where most of his miracles were done, because they did not repent: [21] "Woe to you, Chorazin! Woe to you, Bethsaida! For if the miracles that were done in you had been done in Tyre and Sidon, they would have repented in sackcloth and ashes long ago. [22] But I tell you, it will be more tolerable for Tyre and Sidon on the day of judgment than for you. [23] And you, Capernaum, will you be exalted to heaven? No, you will go down to Hades. For if the miracles that were done in you had been done in Sodom, it would have remained until today. [24] But I tell you, it will be more tolerable for the land of Sodom on the day of judgment than for you."

The Son Gives Knowledge and Rest
[25] At that time Jesus said, "I praise you, Father, Lord of heaven and earth, because you have hidden these things from the wise and intelligent and revealed them to infants. [26] Yes, Father, because this was your good pleasure. [27] All things have been entrusted to me by my Father. No one knows the Son except the Father, and no one knows the Father except the Son and anyone to whom the Son desires to reveal him.

[28] "Come to me, all of you who are weary and burdened, and I will give you rest. [29] Take up my yoke and learn from me, because I am lowly and humble in heart, and you will find rest for your souls. [30] For my yoke is easy and my burden is light."

ISAIAH 29:18-19

[18] On that day the deaf will hear
the words of a document,
and out of a deep darkness
the eyes of the blind will see.
[19] The humble will have joy
after joy in the LORD,
and the poor people will rejoice
in the Holy One of Israel.

1 JOHN 5:3-4

[3] For this is what love for God is: to keep his commands. And his commands are not a burden, [4] because everyone who has been born of God conquers the world. This is the victory that has conquered the world: our faith.

OBSERVE   *What is happening in the text?*

REFLECT   *What does it teach me about Jesus?*

APPLY   *What is my response?*

Why Are There Four Gospels?

The word *gospel* means "good news." A Gospel in the Bible is a book dedicated to telling the story of the life, death, and resurrection of Jesus Christ. Since the early days of Christianity, the Church has recognized four Gospels as giving reliable accounts of the story of Christ: Matthew, Mark, Luke, and John. But why does the Bible include four accounts?

Each Gospel verifies the authenticity of the others. The four writers had a strong connection to Jesus, either as an apostle or someone close to an apostle. The varied accounts help us see Jesus from a few different perspectives, giving us a fuller picture of who He is than we would get from only one account.

ORIGINAL AUDIENCE

MATTHEW	Jews
MARK	Romans
LUKE	Most honorable Theophilus
JOHN	Everyone

PRESENTS JESUS AS	SOME UNIQUE FEATURES
The fulfillment of the Old Testament promise of the Son of David (Matthew 9:27; 21:9)	The Beatitudes, the Five Discourses, many parables
The servant of God (Mark 10:45)	Fast-paced, focused on the narrative
The awaited Messiah (Luke 1:1–4)	Lengthy nativity story, focused on historical detail, includes extended narratives
The divine Son of God (John 1:14)	Poetic voice, a series of "I Am" statements, focused on the last week of Jesus' life

Day 11:
Jesus Is Lord
of the Sabbath

MATTHEW 12

Lord of the Sabbath

[1] At that time Jesus passed through the grainfields on the Sabbath. His disciples were hungry and began to pick and eat some heads of grain. [2] When the Pharisees saw this, they said to him, "See, your disciples are doing what is not lawful to do on the Sabbath."

[3] He said to them, "Haven't you read what David did when he and those who were with him were hungry: [4] how he entered the house of God, and they ate the bread of the Presence—which is not lawful for him or for those with him to eat, but only for the priests? [5] Or haven't you read in the law that on Sabbath days the priests in the temple violate the Sabbath and are innocent? [6] I tell you that something greater than the temple is here. [7] If you had known what this means, I desire mercy and not sacrifice, you would not have condemned the innocent. [8] For the Son of Man is Lord of the Sabbath."

The Man with the Shriveled Hand

[9] Moving on from there, he entered their synagogue. [10] There he saw a man who had a shriveled hand, and in order to accuse him they asked him, "Is it lawful to heal on the Sabbath?"

[11] He replied to them, "Who among you, if he had a sheep that fell into a pit on the Sabbath, wouldn't take hold of it and lift it out? [12] A person is worth far more than a sheep; so it is lawful to do what is good on the Sabbath."

[13] Then he told the man, "Stretch out your hand." So he stretched it out, and it was restored, as good as the other. [14] But the Pharisees went out and plotted against him, how they might kill him.

The Servant of the Lord

[15] Jesus was aware of this and withdrew. Large crowds followed him, and he healed them all. [16] He warned them not to make him known, [17] so that what was spoken through the prophet Isaiah might be fulfilled:

continued

SEA OF GALILEE

¹⁸ Here is my servant whom I have chosen,
my beloved in whom I delight;
I will put my Spirit on him,
and he will proclaim justice to the nations.
¹⁹ He will not argue or shout,
and no one will hear his voice in the streets.
²⁰ He will not break a bruised reed,
and he will not put out a smoldering wick,
until he has led justice to victory.
²¹ The nations will put their hope in his name.

A House Divided

²² Then a demon-possessed man who was blind and unable to speak was brought to him. He healed him, so that the man could both speak and see. ²³ All the crowds were astounded and said, "Could this be the Son of David?"

²⁴ When the Pharisees heard this, they said, "This man drives out demons only by Beelzebul, the ruler of the demons."

²⁵ Knowing their thoughts, he told them: "Every kingdom divided against itself is headed for destruction, and no city or house divided against itself will stand. ²⁶ If Satan drives out Satan, he is divided against himself. How then will his kingdom stand? ²⁷ And if I drive out demons by Beelzebul, by whom do your sons drive them out? For this reason they will be your judges. ²⁸ If I drive out demons by the Spirit of God, then the kingdom of God has come upon you. ²⁹ How can someone enter a strong man's house and steal his possessions unless he first ties up the strong man? Then he can plunder his house. ³⁰ Anyone who is not with me is against me, and anyone who does not gather with me scatters. ³¹ Therefore, I tell you, people will be forgiven every sin and blasphemy, but the blasphemy against the Spirit will not be forgiven. ³² Whoever speaks a word against the Son of Man, it will be forgiven him; but whoever speaks against the Holy Spirit, it will not be forgiven him, either in this age or in the one to come.

A Tree and Its Fruit

³³ "Either make the tree good and its fruit will be good, or make the tree bad and its fruit will be bad; for a tree is known by its fruit. ³⁴ Brood of vipers! How can you speak good things when you are evil? For the mouth speaks from the

"Anyone who is not with me is against me."

12:30

overflow of the heart. [35] A good person produces good things from his storeroom of good, and an evil person produces evil things from his storeroom of evil. [36] I tell you that on the day of judgment people will have to account for every careless word they speak. [37] For by your words you will be acquitted, and by your words you will be condemned."

The Sign of Jonah

[38] Then some of the **scribes** and Pharisees said to him, "Teacher, we want to see a sign from you."

[39] He answered them, "An evil and adulterous generation demands a sign, but no sign will be given to it except the sign of the prophet Jonah. [40] For as Jonah was in the belly of the huge fish three days and three nights, so the Son of Man will be in the heart of the earth three days and three nights. [41] The men of Nineveh will stand up at the judgment with this generation and condemn it, because they repented at Jonah's preaching; and look— something greater than Jonah is here. [42] The queen of the south will rise up at the judgment with this generation and condemn it, because she came from the ends of the earth to hear the wisdom of Solomon; and look—something greater than Solomon is here.

SCRIBES

Largely made up of Pharisees

Professional group trained in copying and interpreting the Law of Moses

Led the plan to kill Jesus

An Unclean Spirit's Return

[43] "When an unclean spirit comes out of a person, it roams through waterless places looking for rest but doesn't find any. [44] Then it says, 'I'll go back to my house that I came from.' Returning, it finds the house vacant, swept, and put in order. [45] Then it goes and brings with it seven other spirits more evil than itself, and they enter and settle down there. As a result, that person's last condition is worse than the first. That's how it will also be with this evil generation."

True Relationships

[46] While he was still speaking with the crowds, his mother and brothers were standing outside wanting to speak to him. [47] Someone told him, "Look, your mother and your brothers are standing outside, wanting to speak to you."

[48] He replied to the one who was speaking to him, "Who is my mother and who are my brothers?" [49] Stretching out his hand toward his disciples, he said, "Here are my mother and my brothers! [50] For whoever does the will of my Father in heaven is my brother and sister and mother."

LEVITICUS 19:9-10

[9] When you reap the harvest of your land, you are not to reap to the very edge of your field or gather the gleanings of your harvest. [10] Do not strip your vineyard bare or gather its fallen grapes. Leave them for the poor and the resident alien; I am the LORD your God.

ISAIAH 42:1–4

The Servant's Mission

[1] This is my servant; I strengthen him,
this is my chosen one; I delight in him.
I have put my Spirit on him;
he will bring justice to the nations.
[2] He will not cry out or shout
or make his voice heard in the streets.
[3] He will not break a bruised reed,
and he will not put out a smoldering wick;
he will faithfully bring justice.
[4] He will not grow weak or be discouraged
until he has established justice on earth.
The coasts and islands will wait for his instruction.

OBSERVE   *What is happening in the text?*

REFLECT   *What does it teach me about Jesus?*

APPLY   *What is my response?*

Day 12: Jesus Speaks in Parables

MATTHEW 13:1-52

The Parable of the Sower

¹ On that day Jesus went out of the house and was sitting by the sea. ² Such large crowds gathered around him that he got into a boat and sat down, while the whole crowd stood on the shore.

³ Then he told them many things in parables, saying: "Consider the sower who went out to sow. ⁴ As he sowed, some seed fell along the path, and the birds came and devoured them. ⁵ Other seed fell on rocky ground where it didn't have much soil, and it grew up quickly since the soil wasn't deep. ⁶ But when the sun came up, it was scorched, and since it had no root, it withered away. ⁷ Other seed fell among thorns, and the thorns came up and choked it. ⁸ Still other seed fell on good ground and produced fruit: some a hundred, some sixty, and some thirty times what was sown. ⁹ Let anyone who has ears listen."

Why Jesus Used Parables

¹⁰ Then the disciples came up and asked him, "Why are you speaking to them in parables?"

¹¹ He answered, "Because the secrets of the kingdom of heaven have been given for you to know, but it has not been given to them. ¹² For whoever has, more will be given to him, and he will have more than enough; but whoever does not have, even what he has will be taken away from him. ¹³ That is why I speak to them in parables, because looking they do not see, and hearing they do not listen or understand. ¹⁴ Isaiah's prophecy is fulfilled in them, which says:

You will listen and listen,
but never understand;
you will look and look,
but never perceive.
¹⁵ For this people's heart has grown callous;
their ears are hard of hearing,
and they have shut their eyes;
otherwise they might see with their eyes,
and hear with their ears, and
understand with their hearts,
and turn back—
and I would heal them.

¹⁶ "Blessed are your eyes because they do see, and your ears because they do hear. ¹⁷ For truly I tell you, many prophets and righteous people longed to see the things you see but didn't see them, to hear the things you hear but didn't hear them.

continued

JERUSALEM, ISRAEL

The Parable of the Sower Explained

18 "So listen to the parable of the sower: 19 When anyone hears the word about the kingdom and doesn't understand it, the evil one comes and snatches away what was sown in his heart. This is the one sown along the path. 20 And the one sown on rocky ground—this is one who hears the word and immediately receives it with joy. 21 But he has no root and is short-lived. When distress or persecution comes because of the word, immediately he falls away. 22 Now the one sown among the thorns—this is one who hears the word, but the worries of this age and the deceitfulness of wealth choke the word, and it becomes unfruitful. 23 But the one sown on the good ground—this is one who hears and understands the word, who does produce fruit and yields: some a hundred, some sixty, some thirty times what was sown."

The Parable of the Wheat and the Weeds

24 He presented another parable to them: "The kingdom of heaven may be compared to a man who sowed good seed in his field. 25 But while people were sleeping, his enemy came, sowed weeds among the wheat, and left. 26 When the plants sprouted and produced grain, then the weeds also appeared. 27 The landowner's servants came to him and said, 'Master, didn't you sow good seed in your field? Then where did the weeds come from?'

28 "'An enemy did this,' he told them.

"'So, do you want us to go and pull them up?' the servants asked him.

29 "'No,' he said. 'When you pull up the weeds, you might also uproot the wheat with them. 30 Let both grow together until the harvest. At harvest time I'll tell the reapers: Gather the weeds first and tie them in bundles to burn them, but collect the wheat in my barn.'"

The Parables of the Mustard Seed and of the Leaven

31 He presented another parable to them: "The kingdom of heaven is like a mustard seed that a man took and sowed in his field. 32 It's the smallest of all the seeds, but when grown, it's taller than the garden plants and becomes a tree, so that the birds of the sky come and nest in its branches."

33 He told them another parable: "The kingdom of heaven is like leaven that a woman took and mixed into fifty pounds of flour until all of it was leavened."

Using Parables Fulfills Prophecy

34 Jesus told the crowds all these things in parables, and he did not tell them anything without a parable, 35 so that what was spoken through the prophet might be fulfilled:

I will open my mouth in parables;
I will declare things kept secret
from the foundation of the world.

Jesus Interprets the Parable of the Wheat and the Weeds

36 Then he left the crowds and went into the house. His disciples approached him and said, "Explain to us the parable of the weeds in the field."

37 He replied: "The one who sows the good seed is the Son of Man; 38 the field is the world; and the good seed—these are the children of the kingdom. The weeds are the children of the evil one, 39 and the enemy who sowed them is the devil. The harvest is the end of the age, and the harvesters are angels. 40 Therefore, just as the weeds are gathered and burned in the fire, so it will be at the end of the age. 41 The Son of Man will send out his angels, and they will gather from his kingdom all who cause sin and those guilty of lawlessness. 42 They will throw them into the blazing furnace where there

"When he found one priceless pearl, he went and sold everything he had and bought it." 13:46

will be weeping and gnashing of teeth. [43] Then the righteous will shine like the sun in their Father's kingdom. Let anyone who has ears listen.

The Parables of the Hidden Treasure and of the Priceless Pearl
[44] "The kingdom of heaven is like treasure, buried in a field, that a man found and reburied. Then in his joy he goes and sells everything he has and buys that field.

[45] "Again, the kingdom of heaven is like a merchant in search of fine pearls. [46] When he found one priceless pearl, he went and sold everything he had and bought it.

The Parable of the Net
[47] "Again, the kingdom of heaven is like a large net thrown into the sea. It collected every kind of fish, [48] and when it was full, they dragged it ashore, sat down, and gathered the good fish into containers, but threw out the worthless ones. [49] So it will be at the end of the age. The angels will go out, separate the evil people from the righteous, [50] and throw them into the blazing furnace, where there will be weeping and gnashing of teeth.

The Storehouse of Truth
[51] "Have you understood all these things?"

They answered him, "Yes."

[52] "Therefore," he said to them, "every teacher of the law who has become a disciple in the kingdom of heaven is like the owner of a house who brings out of his storeroom treasures new and old."

1 CORINTHIANS 5:6-7

[6] Your boasting is not good. Don't you know that a little leaven leavens the whole batch of dough? [7] Clean out the old leaven so that you may be a new unleavened batch, as indeed you are. For Christ our Passover lamb has been sacrificed.

OBSERVE   *What is happening in the text?*

REFLECT   *What does it teach me about Jesus?*

APPLY   *What is my response?*

Day 13:
Grace Day

Use this day to pray, rest, and reflect on this week's reading, giving thanks for the grace that is ours in Christ.

Isaiah 29:18–19

ON THAT DAY THE DEAF WILL HEAR
THE WORDS OF A DOCUMENT,
AND OUT OF A DEEP DARKNESS
THE EYES OF THE BLIND WILL SEE.
THE HUMBLE WILL HAVE JOY
AFTER JOY IN THE LORD,
AND THE POOR PEOPLE WILL REJOICE
IN THE HOLY ONE OF ISRAEL.

Day 14:
Weekly Truth

Scripture is God-breathed and true. When we memorize it, we carry the good news of the gospel of Jesus with us wherever we go.

This week we will memorize a verse from Matthew that powerfully summarizes what Jesus came to do, and why.

Matthew 9:13

"Go and learn what this means: 'I desire mercy and not sacrifice.' For I didn't come to call the righteous, but sinners."

Day 15:
Jesus Is the
Son of God

MATTHEW 13:53–58

Rejection at Nazareth

⁵³ When Jesus had finished these parables, he left there. ⁵⁴ He went to his hometown and began to teach them in their synagogue, so that they were astonished and said, "Where did this man get this wisdom and these miraculous powers? ⁵⁵ Isn't this the carpenter's son? Isn't his mother called Mary, and his brothers **James**, Joseph, Simon, and Judas? ⁵⁶ And his sisters, aren't they all with us? So where does he get all these things?" ⁵⁷ And they were offended by him.

Jesus said to them, "A prophet is not without honor except in his hometown and in his household." ⁵⁸ And he did not do many miracles there because of their unbelief.

MATTHEW 14

John the Baptist Beheaded

¹ At that time **Herod the tetrarch** heard the report about Jesus. ² "This is John the Baptist," he told his servants. "He has been raised from the dead, and that's why miraculous powers are at work in him."

³ For Herod had arrested John, chained him, and put him **in prison** on account of Herodias, his brother Philip's wife, ⁴ since John had been telling him, "It's not lawful for you to have her." ⁵ Though Herod wanted to kill John, he feared the crowd since they regarded John as a prophet.

⁶ When Herod's birthday celebration came, Herodias's daughter danced before them and pleased Herod. ⁷ So he promised with an oath to give her whatever she asked. ⁸ Prompted by her mother, she answered, "Give me John the Baptist's head here on a platter." ⁹ Although the king regretted it, he commanded that it be granted because of his oaths and his guests. ¹⁰ So he sent orders and had John beheaded in the prison. ¹¹ His head was brought on a platter and given to the girl, who carried it to her mother. ¹² Then his disciples came, removed the corpse, buried it, and went and reported to Jesus.

Feeding of the Five Thousand

¹³ When Jesus heard about it, he withdrew from there by boat to a remote place to be alone. When the crowds heard this, they followed him on foot from the towns. ¹⁴ When he went ashore, he saw a large crowd, had compassion on them, and healed their sick.

¹⁵ When evening came, the disciples approached him and said, "This place is deserted, and it is already late. Send the crowds away so that they can go into the villages and buy food for themselves."

MACHAERUS

continued

SEA OF GALILEE

[16] "They don't need to go away," Jesus told them. "You give them something to eat."

[17] "But we only have five loaves and two fish here," they said to him.

[18] "Bring them here to me," he said. [19] Then he commanded the crowds to sit down on the grass. He took the five loaves and the two fish, and looking up to heaven, he blessed them. He broke the loaves and gave them to the disciples, and the disciples gave them to the crowds. [20] Everyone ate and was satisfied. They picked up twelve baskets full of leftover pieces. [21] Now those who ate were about five thousand men, besides women and children.

Walking on the Water

[22] Immediately he made the disciples get into the boat and go ahead of him to the other side, while he dismissed the crowds. [23] After dismissing the crowds, he went up on the mountain by himself to pray. Well into the night, he was there alone. [24] Meanwhile, the boat was already some distance from land, battered by the waves, because the wind was against them. [25] Jesus came toward them walking on the sea very early in the morning. [26] When the disciples saw him walking on the sea, they were terrified. "It's a ghost!" they said, and they cried out in fear.

[27] Immediately Jesus spoke to them. "Have courage! It is I. Don't be afraid."

[28] "Lord, if it's you," Peter answered him, "command me to come to you on the water."

[29] He said, "Come."

And climbing out of the boat, Peter started walking on the water and came toward Jesus. [30] But when he saw the strength of the wind, he was afraid, and beginning to sink he cried out, "Lord, save me!"

[31] Immediately Jesus reached out his hand, caught hold of him, and said to him, "You of little faith, why did you doubt?"

[32] When they got into the boat, the wind ceased. [33] Then those in the boat worshiped him and said, "Truly you are the Son of God."

Miraculous Healings

[34] When they had crossed over, they came to shore at Gennesaret. [35] When the men of that place recognized him, they alerted the whole vicinity and brought to him all who were sick. [36] They begged him that they might only touch the end of his robe, and as many as touched it were healed.

DEUTERONOMY 8:3

He humbled you by letting you go hungry; then he gave you manna to eat, which you and your fathers had not known, so that you might learn that man does not live on bread alone but on every word that comes from the mouth of the Lord.

ISAIAH 43:10-13

[10] "You are my witnesses"—
　　this is the Lord's declaration—
"and my servant whom I have chosen,
so that you may know and believe me
and understand that I am he.
No god was formed before me,
and there will be none after me.
[11] I—I am the Lord.
Besides me, there is no Savior.
[12] I alone declared, saved, and proclaimed—
and not some foreign god among you.
So you are my witnesses"—
　　this is the Lord's declaration—
"and I am God.
[13] Also, from today on I am he alone,
and none can rescue from my power.
I act, and who can reverse it?"

OBSERVE   *What is happening in the text?*

REFLECT   *What does it teach me about Jesus?*

APPLY   *What is my response?*

Day 16:
Jesus Is the
Messiah

MATTHEW 15

The Tradition of the Elders

[1] Then Jesus was approached by Pharisees and scribes from Jerusalem, who asked, [2] "Why do your disciples break the tradition of the elders? For they don't wash their hands when they eat."

[3] He answered them, "Why do you break God's commandment because of your tradition? [4] For God said: Honor your father and your mother; and, Whoever speaks evil of father or mother must be put to death. [5] But you say, 'Whoever tells his father or mother, "Whatever benefit you might have received from me is a gift committed to the temple," [6] he does not have to honor his father.' In this way, you have nullified the word of God because of your tradition. [7] Hypocrites! Isaiah prophesied correctly about you when he said:

[8] This people honors me with their lips,
but their heart is far from me.
[9] They worship me in vain,
teaching as doctrines human commands."

Defilement Is from Within

[10] Summoning the crowd, he told them, "Listen and understand: [11] It's not what goes into the mouth that defiles a person, but what comes out of the mouth—this defiles a person."

[12] Then the disciples came up and told him, "Do you know that the Pharisees took offense when they heard what you said?"

[13] He replied, "Every plant that my heavenly Father didn't plant will be uprooted. [14] Leave them alone! They are blind guides. And if the blind guide the blind, both will fall into a pit."

[15] Then Peter said, "Explain this parable to us."

[16] "Do you still lack understanding?" he asked. [17] "Don't you realize that whatever goes into the mouth passes into the stomach and is eliminated? [18] But what comes out of the mouth comes from the heart, and this defiles a person. [19] For from the heart come evil thoughts, murders, adulteries, sexual immoralities, thefts, false testimonies, slander. [20] These are the things that defile a person; but eating with unwashed hands does not defile a person."

continued

WADI QELT

TYRE & SIDON

A Gentile Mother's Faith

[21] When Jesus left there, he withdrew to the area of **Tyre and Sidon**. [22] Just then a Canaanite woman from that region came and kept crying out, "Have mercy on me, Lord, Son of David! My daughter is severely tormented by a demon."

[23] Jesus did not say a word to her. His disciples approached him and urged him, "Send her away because she's crying out after us."

[24] He replied, "I was sent only to the lost sheep of the house of Israel."

[25] But she came, knelt before him, and said, "Lord, help me!"

[26] He answered, "It isn't right to take the children's bread and throw it to the dogs."

[27] "Yes, Lord," she said, "yet even the dogs eat the crumbs that fall from their masters' table."

[28] Then Jesus replied to her, "Woman, your faith is great. Let it be done for you as you want." And from that moment her daughter was healed.

Healing Many People

[29] Moving on from there, Jesus passed along the Sea of Galilee. He went up on a mountain and sat there, [30] and large crowds came to him, including the lame, the blind, the crippled, those unable to speak, and many others. They put them at his feet, and he healed them. [31] So the crowd was amazed when they saw those unable to speak talking, the crippled restored, the lame walking, and the blind seeing, and they gave glory to the God of Israel.

Feeding of the Four Thousand

[32] Jesus called his disciples and said, "I have compassion on the crowd, because they've already stayed with me three days and have nothing to eat. I don't want to send them away hungry, otherwise they might collapse on the way."

[33] The disciples said to him, "Where could we get enough bread in this desolate place to feed such a crowd?"

[34] "How many loaves do you have?" Jesus asked them.

"Seven," they said, "and a few small fish."

[35] After commanding the crowd to sit down on the ground, [36] he took the seven loaves and the fish, gave thanks, broke them, and gave them to the disciples, and the disciples gave them to the crowds. [37] They all ate and were satisfied. They collected the leftover pieces—seven large baskets full. [38] Now there were four thousand men who had eaten, besides women and children. [39] After dismissing the crowds, he got into the boat and went to the region of **Magadan**.

MAGADAN

The Leaven of the Pharisees and the Sadducees

[1] The Pharisees and Sadducees approached, and tested him, asking him to show them a sign from heaven. [2] He replied, "When evening comes you say, 'It will be good weather because the sky is red.' [3] And in the morning, 'Today will be stormy because the sky is red and threatening.' You know how to read the appearance of the sky, but you can't read the signs of the times. [4] An evil and adulterous generation demands a sign, but no sign will be given to it except the sign of Jonah." Then he left them and went away.

[5] The disciples reached the other shore, and they had forgotten to take bread. [6] Then Jesus told them, "Watch out and beware of the leaven of the Pharisees and Sadducees."

[7] They were discussing among themselves, "We didn't bring any bread."

[8] Aware of this, Jesus said, "You of little faith, why are you discussing among yourselves that you do not have bread? [9] Don't you understand yet? Don't you remember the five loaves for the five thousand and how many baskets you collected? [10] Or the seven loaves for the four thousand and how many large baskets you collected? [11] Why is it you don't understand that when I told you, 'Beware of the leaven of the Pharisees and Sadducees,' it wasn't about bread?" [12] Then they understood that he had not told them to beware of the leaven in bread, but of the teaching of the Pharisees and Sadducees.

Peter's Confession of the Messiah

[13] When Jesus came to the region of **Caesarea Philippi**, he asked his disciples, "Who do people say that the Son of Man is?"

[14] They replied, "Some say John the Baptist; others, Elijah; still others, Jeremiah or one of the prophets."

[15] "But you," he asked them, "who do you say that I am?"

[16] Simon Peter answered, "You are the Messiah, the Son of the living God."

[17] Jesus responded, "Blessed are you, Simon son of Jonah, because flesh and blood did not reveal this to you, but my Father in heaven. [18] And I also say to you that you are Peter, and on this rock I will build my church, and the gates of Hades will not overpower it. [19] I will give you the keys of the kingdom of heaven, and whatever you bind on earth will have been bound in heaven, and whatever you loose on earth will have been loosed in heaven." [20] Then he gave the disciples orders to tell no one that he was the Messiah.

CAESAREA
PHILIPPI

His Death and Resurrection Predicted

²¹ From then on Jesus began to point out to his disciples that it was necessary for him to go to Jerusalem and suffer many things from the **elders**, chief priests, and scribes, be killed, and be raised the third day. ²² Peter took him aside and began to rebuke him, "Oh no, Lord! This will never happen to you!"

²³ Jesus turned and told Peter, "Get behind me, Satan! You are a hindrance to me because you're not thinking about God's concerns but human concerns."

Take Up Your Cross

²⁴ Then Jesus said to his disciples, "If anyone wants to follow after me, let him deny himself, take up his cross, and follow me. ²⁵ For whoever wants to save his life will lose it, but whoever loses his life because of me will find it. ²⁶ For what will it benefit someone if he gains the whole world yet loses his life? Or what will anyone give in exchange for his life? ²⁷ For the Son of Man is going to come with his angels in the glory of his Father, and then he will reward each according to what he has done. ²⁸ Truly I tell you, there are some standing here who will not taste death until they see the Son of Man coming in his kingdom."

ELDERS OF THE PEOPLE

A council of men from prominent Jewish families

Part of the Sanhedrin

Held leadership role in the government of the local synagogue

ZECHARIAH 12:10

Then I will pour out a spirit of grace and prayer on the house of David and the residents of Jerusalem, and they will look at me whom they pierced. They will mourn for him as one mourns for an only child and weep bitterly for him as one weeps for a firstborn.

2 PETER 1:16-18

The Trustworthy Prophetic Word

¹⁶ For we did not follow cleverly contrived myths when we made known to you the power and coming of our Lord Jesus Christ; instead, we were eyewitnesses of his majesty. ¹⁷ For he received honor and glory from God the Father when the voice came to him from the Majestic Glory, saying "This is my beloved Son, with whom I am well-pleased!" ¹⁸ We ourselves heard this voice when it came from heaven while we were with him on the holy mountain.

OBSERVE   *What is happening in the text?*

REFLECT   *What does it teach me about Jesus?*

APPLY   *What is my response?*

Day 17:
Jesus's Glory
and Power

MATTHEW 17

The Transfiguration

[1] After six days Jesus took Peter, James, and his brother John and led them up on a high mountain by themselves. [2] He was transfigured in front of them, and his face shone like the sun; his clothes became as white as the light. [3] Suddenly, Moses and Elijah appeared to them, talking with him. [4] Then Peter said to Jesus, "Lord, it's good for us to be here. I will set up three shelters here: one for you, one for Moses, and one for Elijah."

[5] While he was still speaking, suddenly a bright cloud covered them, and a voice from the cloud said: "This is my beloved Son, with whom I am well-pleased. Listen to him!" [6] When the disciples heard this, they fell facedown and were terrified.

[7] Jesus came up, touched them, and said, "Get up; don't be afraid." [8] When they looked up they saw no one except Jesus alone.

[9] As they were coming down the mountain, Jesus commanded them, "Don't tell anyone about the vision until the Son of Man is raised from the dead."

[10] So the disciples asked him, "Why then do the scribes say that Elijah must come first?"

[11] "Elijah is coming and will restore everything," he replied. [12] "But I tell you: Elijah has already come, and they didn't recognize him. On the contrary, they did whatever they pleased to him. In the same way the Son of Man is going to suffer at their hands." [13] Then the disciples understood that he had spoken to them about John the Baptist.

The Power of Jesus over a Demon

[14] When they reached the crowd, a man approached and knelt down before him. [15] "Lord," he said, "have mercy on my son, because he has seizures and suffers terribly. He often falls into the fire and often into the water. [16] I brought him to your disciples, but they couldn't heal him."

[17] Jesus replied, "You unbelieving and perverse generation, how long will I be with you? How long must I put up with you? Bring him here to me." [18] Then Jesus rebuked the demon, and it came out of him, and from that moment the boy was healed.

[19] Then the disciples approached Jesus privately and said, "Why couldn't we drive it out?"

[20] "Because of your little faith," he told them. "For truly I tell you, if you have faith the size of a mustard seed, you will tell this mountain, 'Move from here to there,' and it will move. Nothing will be impossible for you."

continued

EIN GEDI, ISRAEL

Matthew's Five Discourses

One of Matthew's key objectives was to collect and present the teachings of Jesus as clearly as possible. One way he did this was by including five extended sections of teaching in his Gospel, known as Matthew's Five Discourses. For Matthew's mostly Jewish audience, these five discourses would have called to mind the five books of Moses.

THE BASICS OF THE FAITH
Matthew 5–7

An overview of the Christian life and the work of Christ. This discourse, most commonly known as the Sermon on the Mount, discusses the essential aspects of ethics, conduct, and worship for the believer.

- The Beatitudes (5:1–12)
- The characteristics of kingdom righteousness (5:13–48)
- The practice of kingdom righteousness (6:1–7:12)
- Seeking the kingdom of heaven (7:13–29)

THE MISSION OF THE CHURCH
Matthew 10

Instruction directed to Jesus's twelve disciples, preparing them for their calling to take the gospel out into the world.

- Christian ministry (10:1–15)
- Anticipating various responses to that ministry (10:16–42)

THE KINGDOM OF HEAVEN
Matthew 13

A collection of parables focused on imparting Christian wisdom while revealing what the kingdom of heaven will be like.

- The parable of the sower, told and explained (13:1–23)
- Other kingdom parables (13:24–52)
- Responses to Jesus's parables (13:53–58)

THE CHARACTER OF THE CHRISTIAN
Matthew 18

Parables and teaching focused on the coming community of faith and the role the apostles will play in leading it.

- Humility (18:1–20)
- Forgiveness (18:21–35)

THE END OF ALL THINGS
Matthew 24-25

Given near the time of Jesus's crucifixion. This section, usually referred to as the Olivet Discourse, focuses on the judgment that will soon come upon the world and the mercy that is found in Christ alone.

- Prophecy about the coming kingdom (24:1–35)
- Call to readiness (24:36–25:30)
- The promise of coming judgment (25:31–46)

The Second Prediction of His Death

22 As they were gathering together in Galilee, Jesus told them, "The Son of Man is about to be betrayed into the hands of men. 23 They will kill him, and on the third day he will be raised up." And they were deeply distressed.

Paying the Temple Tax

24 When they came to Capernaum, those who collected the temple tax approached Peter and said, "Doesn't your teacher pay the temple tax?"

25 "Yes," he said.

When he went into the house, Jesus spoke to him first, "What do you think, Simon? From whom do earthly kings collect tariffs or taxes? From their sons or from strangers?"

26 "From strangers," he said.

"Then the sons are free," Jesus told him. 27 "But, so we won't offend them, go to the sea, cast in a fishhook, and take the first fish that you catch. When you open its mouth you'll find a coin. Take it and give it to them for me and you."

MATTHEW 18

Who Is the Greatest?

1 At that time the disciples came to Jesus and asked, "So who is greatest in the kingdom of heaven?" 2 He called a child and had him stand among them. 3 "Truly I tell you," he said, "unless you turn and become like children, you will never enter the kingdom of heaven. 4 Therefore, whoever humbles himself like this child—this one is the greatest in the kingdom of heaven. 5 And whoever welcomes one child like this in my name welcomes me.

6 "But whoever causes one of these little ones who believe in me to fall away—it would be better for him if a heavy millstone were hung around his neck and he were drowned in the depths of the sea. 7 Woe to the world because of offenses. For offenses will inevitably come, but woe to that person by whom the offense comes. 8 If your hand or your foot causes you to fall away, cut it off and throw it away. It is better for you to enter life maimed or lame than to have two hands or two feet and be thrown into the eternal fire.

9 And if your eye causes you to fall away, gouge it out and throw it away. It is better for you to enter life with one eye than to have two eyes and be thrown into hellfire.

The Parable of the Lost Sheep

10 "See to it that you don't despise one of these little ones, because I tell you that in heaven their angels continually view the face of my Father in heaven. 12 What do you think? If someone has a hundred sheep, and one of them goes astray, won't he leave the ninety-nine on the hillside and go and search for the stray? 13 And if he finds it, truly I tell you, he rejoices over that sheep more than over the ninety-nine that did not go astray. 14 In the same way, it is not the will of your Father in heaven that one of these little ones perish.

Restoring a Brother

15 "If your brother sins against you, go and rebuke him in private. If he listens to you, you have won your brother. 16 But if he won't listen, take one or two others with you, so that by the testimony of two or three witnesses every fact may be established. 17 If he doesn't pay attention to them, tell the church. If he doesn't pay attention even to the church, let him be like a Gentile and a tax collector to you. 18 Truly I tell you, whatever you bind on earth will have been bound in heaven, and whatever you loose on earth will have been loosed in heaven. 19 Again, truly I tell you, if two of you on earth agree about any matter that you pray for, it will be done for you by my Father in heaven. 20 For where two or three are gathered together in my name, I am there among them."

The Parable of the Unforgiving Servant

21 Then Peter approached him and asked, "Lord, how many times shall I forgive my brother or sister who sins against me? As many as seven times?"

22 "I tell you, not as many as seven," Jesus replied, "but seventy times seven.

23 "For this reason, the kingdom of heaven can be compared to a king who wanted to settle accounts with his servants. 24 When he began to settle accounts, one who owed ten thousand talents was brought before him. 25 Since he did not have the money to pay it back, his master commanded that he, his wife, his children, and everything he had be sold to pay the debt.

26 "At this, the servant fell facedown before him and said, 'Be patient with me, and I will pay you everything.' 27 Then the master of that servant had compassion, released him, and forgave him the loan.

28 "That servant went out and found one of his fellow servants who owed him a hundred denarii. He grabbed him, started choking him, and said, 'Pay what you owe!'

29 "At this, his fellow servant fell down and began begging him, 'Be patient with me, and I will pay you back.' 30 But he wasn't willing. Instead, he went and threw him into prison until he could pay what was owed. 31 When the other servants saw what had taken place, they were deeply distressed and went and reported to their master everything that had happened. 32 Then, after he had summoned him, his master said to him, 'You wicked servant! I forgave you all that debt because you begged me. 33 Shouldn't you also have had mercy on your fellow servant, as I had mercy on you?' 34 And because he was angry, his master handed him over to the jailers to be tortured until he could pay everything that was owed. 35 So also my heavenly Father will do to you unless every one of you forgives his brother or sister from your heart."

1 KINGS 8:10-13

10 When the priests came out of the holy place, the cloud filled the LORD's temple, 11 and because of the cloud, the priests were not able to continue ministering, for the glory of the LORD filled the temple.

12 Then Solomon said:

The LORD said that he would dwell in total darkness.
13 I have indeed built an exalted temple for you,
a place for your dwelling forever.

JEREMIAH 23:1-4

The LORD and His Sheep

1 "Woe to the shepherds who destroy and scatter the sheep of my pasture!" This is the LORD's declaration. 2 "Therefore, this is what the LORD, the God of Israel, says about the shepherds who tend my people: You have scattered my flock, banished them, and have not attended to them. I am about to attend to you because of your evil acts"—this is the LORD's declaration. 3 "I will gather the remnant of my flock from all the lands where I have banished them, and I will return them to their grazing land. They will become fruitful and numerous. 4 I will raise up shepherds over them who will tend them. They will no longer be afraid or discouraged, nor will any be missing." This is the LORD's declaration.

"It is not the will of your Father in heaven that one of these little ones perish."

18:14

OBSERVE   *What is happening in the text?*

REFLECT   *What does it teach me about Jesus?*

APPLY   *What is my response?*

Day 18:
Jesus Came
to Serve

JUDEA ACROSS
THE JORDAN

MATTHEW 19

The Question of Divorce

¹ When Jesus had finished saying these things, he departed from Galilee and went to the region of **Judea across the Jordan**. ² Large crowds followed him, and he healed them there. ³ Some Pharisees approached him to test him. They asked, "Is it lawful for a man to divorce his wife on any grounds?"

⁴ "Haven't you read," he replied, "that he who created them in the beginning made them male and female," ⁵ and he also said, "For this reason a man will leave his father and mother and be joined to his wife, and the two will become one flesh? ⁶ So they are no longer two, but one flesh. Therefore, what God has joined together, let no one separate."

⁷ "Why then," they asked him, "did Moses command us to give divorce papers and to send her away?"

⁸ He told them, "Moses permitted you to divorce your wives because of the hardness of your hearts, but it was not like that from the beginning. ⁹ I tell you, whoever divorces his wife, except for sexual immorality, and marries another commits adultery."

¹⁰ His disciples said to him, "If the relationship of a man with his wife is like this, it's better not to marry."

¹¹ He responded, "Not everyone can accept this saying, but only those to whom it has been given. ¹² For there are eunuchs who were born that way from their mother's womb, there are eunuchs who were made by men, and there are eunuchs who have made themselves that way because of the kingdom of heaven. The one who is able to accept it should accept it."

Blessing the Children

¹³ Then children were brought to Jesus for him to place his hands on them and pray, but the disciples rebuked them. ¹⁴ Jesus said, "Leave the children alone, and don't try to keep them from coming to me, because the kingdom of heaven belongs to such as these." ¹⁵ After placing his hands on them, he went on from there.

The Rich Young Ruler

¹⁶ Just then someone came up and asked him, "Teacher, what good must I do to have eternal life?"

¹⁷ "Why do you ask me about what is good?" he said to him. "There is only one who is good. If you want to enter into life, keep the commandments."

¹⁸ "Which ones?" he asked him.

Jesus answered: Do not murder; do not commit adultery; do not steal; do not bear false witness; ¹⁹ honor your father and your mother; and love your neighbor as yourself.

²⁰ "I have kept all these," the young man told him. "What do I still lack?"

²¹ "If you want to be perfect," Jesus said to him, "go, sell your belongings and give to the poor, and you will have treasure in heaven. Then come, follow me."

²² When the young man heard that, he went away grieving, because he had many possessions.

Possessions and the Kingdom

²³ Jesus said to his disciples, "Truly I tell you, it will be hard for a rich person to enter the kingdom of heaven. ²⁴ Again I tell you, it is easier for a camel to go through the eye of a needle than for a rich person to enter the kingdom of God."

²⁵ When the disciples heard this, they were utterly astonished and asked, "Then who can be saved?"

²⁶ Jesus looked at them and said, "With man this is impossible, but with God all things are possible."

²⁷ Then Peter responded to him, "See, we have left everything and followed you. So what will there be for us?"

²⁸ Jesus said to them, "Truly I tell you, in the renewal of all things, when the Son of Man sits on his glorious throne, you who have followed me will also sit on twelve thrones, judging the twelve tribes of Israel. ²⁹ And everyone who has left houses or brothers or sisters or father or mother or children or fields because of my name will receive a hundred times more and will inherit eternal life. ³⁰ But many who are first will be last, and the last first.

The Parable of the Vineyard Workers

¹ "For the kingdom of heaven is like a landowner who went out early in the morning to hire workers for his vineyard. ² After agreeing with the workers on one denarius, he sent them into his vineyard for the day. ³ When he went out about nine in the morning, he saw others standing in the marketplace doing nothing. ⁴ He said to them, 'You also go into my vineyard, and I'll give you whatever is right.' So off they went. ⁵ About noon and about three, he went out again and did the same thing. ⁶ Then about five he went and found others standing around and said to them, 'Why have you been standing here all day doing nothing?'

⁷ "'Because no one hired us,' they said to him.

"'You also go into my vineyard,' he told them. ⁸ When evening came, the owner of the vineyard told his foreman, 'Call the workers and give them their pay, starting with the last and ending with the first.'

⁹ "When those who were hired about five came, they each received one denarius. ¹⁰ So when the first ones came, they assumed they would get more, but they also received a denarius each. ¹¹ When they received it, they began to complain to the landowner: ¹² 'These last men put in one hour, and you made them equal to us who bore the burden of the day's work and the burning heat.'

¹³ "He replied to one of them, 'Friend, I'm doing you no wrong. Didn't you agree with me on a denarius? ¹⁴ Take what's yours and go. I want to give this last man the same as I gave you. ¹⁵ Don't I have the right to do what I want with what is mine? Are you jealous because I'm generous?'

¹⁶ "So the last will be first, and the first last."

"Then come, follow me." 19:21

The Third Prediction of His Death

¹⁷ While going up to Jerusalem, Jesus took the twelve disciples aside privately and said to them on the way, ¹⁸ "See, we are going up to Jerusalem. The Son of Man will be handed over to the **chief priests** and scribes, and they will condemn him to death. ¹⁹ They will hand him over to the Gentiles to be mocked, flogged, and crucified, and on the third day he will be raised. "

Suffering and Service

²⁰ Then **the mother of Zebedee's sons** approached him with her sons. She knelt down to ask him for something. ²¹ "What do you want?" he asked her.

"Promise," she said to him, "that these two sons of mine may sit, one on your right and the other on your left, in your kingdom."

²² Jesus answered, "You don't know what you're asking. Are you able to drink the cup that I am about to drink?"

"We are able," they said to him.

²³ He told them, "You will indeed drink my cup, but to sit at my right and left is not mine to give; instead, it is for those for whom it has been prepared by my Father."

²⁴ When the ten disciples heard this, they became indignant with the two brothers. ²⁵ Jesus called them over and said, "You know that the rulers of the Gentiles lord it over them, and those in high positions act as tyrants over them. ²⁶ It must not be like that among you. On the contrary, whoever wants to become great among you must be your servant, ²⁷ and whoever wants to be first among you must be your slave; ²⁸ just as the Son of Man did not come to be served, but to serve, and to give his life as a ransom for many."

Two Blind Men Healed

²⁹ As they were leaving **Jericho**, a large crowd followed him. ³⁰ There were two blind men sitting by the road. When they heard that Jesus was passing by, they cried out, "Lord, have mercy on us, Son of David!" ³¹ The crowd demanded that they keep quiet, but they cried out all the more, "Lord, have mercy on us, Son of David!"

³² Jesus stopped, called them, and said, "What do you want me to do for you?"

³³ "Lord," they said to him, "open our eyes." ³⁴ Moved with compassion, Jesus touched their eyes. Immediately they could see, and they followed him.

PRIESTS /
CHIEF PRIESTS /
HIGH PRIESTS

Official worship leaders for the Jewish people

Represented Israel before God and offered sacrifices on behalf of the people

The most powerful Jews in Jerusalem

JERICHO

DEUTERONOMY 6:4

Listen, Israel: The LORD our God, the LORD is one.

2 PETER 3:10–13

[10] But the day of the Lord will come like a thief; on that day the heavens will pass away with a loud noise, the elements will burn and be dissolved, and the earth and the works on it will be disclosed. [11] Since all these things are to be dissolved in this way, it is clear what sort of people you should be in holy conduct and godliness [12] as you wait for the day of God and hasten its coming. Because of that day, the heavens will be dissolved with fire and the elements will melt with heat. [13] But based on his promise, we wait for new heavens and a new earth, where righteousness dwells.

OBSERVE   *What is happening in the text?*

REFLECT   *What does it teach me about Jesus?*

APPLY   *What is my response?*

"Lord," they said to him, "Open our eyes."

20:33

Day 19:
Jesus Is King

BETHPAGE

JERUSALEM

The Triumphal Entry

¹ When they approached Jerusalem and came to **Bethphage** at the Mount of Olives, Jesus then sent two disciples, ² telling them, "Go into the village ahead of you. At once you will find a donkey tied there with her foal. Untie them and bring them to me. ³ If anyone says anything to you, say that the Lord needs them, and he will send them at once."

⁴ This took place so that what was spoken through the prophet might be fulfilled:

⁵ Tell Daughter Zion,
"See, your King is coming to you,
gentle, and mounted on a donkey,
and on a colt,
the foal of a donkey."

⁶ The disciples went and did just as Jesus directed them. ⁷ They brought the donkey and its foal; then they laid their clothes on them, and he sat on them. ⁸ A very large crowd spread their clothes on the road; others were cutting branches from the trees and spreading them on the road. ⁹ Then the crowds who went ahead of him and those who followed shouted:

Hosanna to the Son of David!
Blessed is he who comes in the name
of the Lord!
Hosanna in the highest heaven!

¹⁰ When he entered **Jerusalem**, the whole city was in an uproar, saying, "Who is this?" ¹¹ The crowds were saying, "This is the prophet Jesus from Nazareth in Galilee."

Cleansing the Temple

¹² Jesus went into the temple and threw out all those buying and selling. He overturned the tables of the **money changers** and the chairs of those selling doves. ¹³ He said to them, "It is written, my house will be called a house of prayer, but you are making it a den of thieves!"

Children Praise Jesus

¹⁴ The blind and the lame came to him in the temple, and he healed them. ¹⁵ When the chief priests and the scribes saw the wonders that he did and the children shouting in the temple, "Hosanna to the Son of David!" they were indignant ¹⁶ and said to him, "Do you hear what these children are saying?"

MONEY CHANGERS

Responsible for exchanging other currencies for Jewish money

Set up tables in the temple so worshipers could get the correct currency to pay the temple tax and buy sacrifices

Often profited greatly by charging interest rates ranging from 20% to 300%

Week Three

Jesus replied, "Yes, have you never read:

> You have prepared praise
> from the mouths of infants and nursing babies?"

[17] Then he left them, went out of the city to Bethany, and spent the night there.

The Barren Fig Tree

[18] Early in the morning, as he was returning to the city, he was hungry. [19] Seeing a lone fig tree by the road, he went up to it and found nothing on it except leaves. And he said to it, "May no fruit ever come from you again!" At once the fig tree withered.

[20] When the disciples saw it, they were amazed and said, "How did the fig tree wither so quickly?"

[21] Jesus answered them, "Truly I tell you, if you have faith and do not doubt, you will not only do what was done to the fig tree, but even if you tell this mountain, 'Be lifted up and thrown into the sea,' it will be done. [22] And if you believe, you will receive whatever you ask for in prayer."

The Authority of Jesus Challenged

[23] When he entered the temple, the chief priests and the elders of the people came to him as he was teaching and said, "By what authority are you doing these things? Who gave you this authority?"

[24] Jesus answered them, "I will also ask you one question, and if you answer it for me, then I will tell you by what authority I do these things. [25] Did John's baptism come from heaven, or was it of human origin?"

They discussed it among themselves, "If we say, 'From heaven,' he will say to us, 'Then why didn't you believe him?' [26] But if we say, 'Of human origin,' we're afraid of the crowd, because everyone considers John to be a prophet." [27] So they answered Jesus, "We don't know."

And he said to them, "Neither will I tell you by what authority I do these things.

The Parable of the Two Sons
[28] "What do you think? A man had two sons. He went to the first and said, 'My son, go work in the vineyard today.'

[29] "He answered, 'I don't want to,' but later he changed his mind and went. [30] Then the man went to the other and said the same thing. 'I will, sir,' he answered, but he didn't go. [31] Which of the two did his father's will?"

They said, "The first."

Jesus said to them, "Truly I tell you, tax collectors and prostitutes are entering the kingdom of God before you. [32] For John came to you in the way of righteousness, and you didn't believe him. Tax collectors and prostitutes did believe him; but you, when you saw it, didn't even change your minds then and believe him.

The Parable of the Vineyard Owner
[33] "Listen to another parable: There was a landowner, who planted a vineyard, put a fence around it, dug a winepress in it, and built a watchtower. He leased it to tenant farmers and went away. [34] When the time came to harvest fruit, he sent his servants to the farmers to collect his fruit. [35] The farmers took his servants, beat one, killed another, and stoned a third. [36] Again, he sent other servants, more than the first group, and they did the same to them. [37] Finally, he sent his son to them. 'They will respect my son,' he said.

[38] "But when the tenant farmers saw the son, they said to each other, 'This is the heir. Come, let's kill him and take his inheritance.' [39] So they seized him, threw him out of the vineyard, and killed him. [40] Therefore, when the owner of the vineyard comes, what will he do to those farmers?"

[41] "He will completely destroy those terrible men," they told him, "and lease his vineyard to other farmers who will give him his fruit at the harvest."

[42] Jesus said to them, "Have you never read in the Scriptures:

The stone that the builders rejected
has become the cornerstone.
This is what the LORD has done
and it is wonderful in our eyes?

[43] Therefore I tell you, the kingdom of God will be taken away from you and given to a people producing its fruit. [44] Whoever falls on this stone will be broken to pieces; but on whomever it falls, it will shatter him."

[45] When the chief priests and the Pharisees heard his parables, they knew he was speaking about them. [46] Although they were looking for a way to arrest him, they feared the crowds, because the people regarded him as a prophet.

EZEKIEL 16:10–13

[10] I clothed you in embroidered cloth and provided you with fine leather sandals. I also wrapped you in fine linen and covered you with silk. [11] I adorned you with jewelry, putting bracelets on your wrists and a necklace around your neck. [12] I put a ring in your nose, earrings on your ears, and a beautiful crown on your head. [13] So you were adorned with gold and silver, and your clothing was made of fine linen, silk, and embroidered cloth. You ate fine flour, honey, and oil. You became extremely beautiful and attained royalty.

ZECHARIAH 9:9

Rejoice greatly, Daughter Zion!
Shout in triumph, Daughter Jerusalem!
Look, your King is coming to you;
he is righteous and victorious,
humble and riding on a donkey,
on a colt, the foal of a donkey.

OBSERVE   *What is happening in the text?*

REFLECT   *What does it teach me about Jesus?*

APPLY   *What is my response?*

Day 20:
Grace Day

Use this day to pray, rest, and reflect on this week's reading, giving thanks for the grace that is ours in Christ.

Isaiah 43:11–12

"I—I AM THE LORD.
BESIDES ME, THERE IS NO SAVIOR.
I ALONE DECLARED, SAVED, AND PROCLAIMED—
AND NOT SOME FOREIGN GOD AMONG YOU.
SO YOU ARE MY WITNESSES"—
THIS IS THE LORD'S DECLARATION—
"AND I AM GOD."

Day 21:
Weekly Truth

Matthew 20:28

"The Son of Man did not come to be served, but to serve, and to give his life as a ransom for many."

COME, YE SINNERS, POOR AND NEEDY

Verses: Joseph Hart (1712-1768)
Refrain: Anonymous
Tune: Walker's Southern Harmony

MATTHEW: THIS IS JESUS

1. Come ye sin - ners, poor and nee - dy, Weak and woun - ded, sick and sore;
2. Come, ye thir - sty, come and wel - come, God's free boun - ty glo - ri - fy;
3. Come ye wea - ry, hea - vy - la - den, Lost and ru - ined by the fall;
4. Let not cons - cience make you lin - ger, Nor of fit - ness fond - ly dream;

Je - sus read - y stands to save you, Full of pi - ty, love and pow'r.
True be - lief and true re - pen - tance, Ev' - ry grace that brings you nigh.
If you tar - ry till you're bet - ter, You will ne - ver come at all.
All the fit - ness He re - qui - reth Is to feel your need of Him.

Chorus

I will a - rise and go to Je - sus, He will em - brace me in His arms;

In the arms of my dear Sa - vior, O there are ten thou - sand charms.

ARAD, ISRAEL

Day 22:
Jesus Is Our
Access to God

MATTHEW 22

The Parable of the Wedding Banquet

[1] Once more Jesus spoke to them in parables: [2] "The kingdom of heaven is like a king who gave a wedding banquet for his son. [3] He sent his servants to summon those invited to the banquet, but they didn't want to come. [4] Again, he sent out other servants and said, 'Tell those who are invited: See, I've prepared my dinner; my oxen and fattened cattle have been slaughtered, and everything is ready. Come to the wedding banquet.'

[5] "But they paid no attention and went away, one to his own farm, another to his business, [6] while the rest seized his servants, mistreated them, and killed them. [7] The king was enraged, and he sent out his troops, killed those murderers, and burned down their city.

[8] "Then he told his servants, 'The banquet is ready, but those who were invited were not worthy. [9] Go then to where the roads exit the city and invite everyone you find to the banquet.' [10] So those servants went out on the roads and gathered everyone they found, both evil and good. The wedding banquet was filled with guests. [11] When the king came in to see the guests, he saw a man there who was not dressed for a wedding. [12] So he said to him, 'Friend, how did you get in here without wedding clothes?' The man was speechless.

[13] "Then the king told the attendants, 'Tie him up hand and foot, and throw him into the outer darkness, where there will be weeping and gnashing of teeth.'

[14] "For many are invited, but few are chosen."

God and Caesar

[15] Then the Pharisees went and plotted how to trap him by what he said. [16] So they sent their disciples to him, along with the **Herodians**. "Teacher," they said, "we know that you are truthful and teach truthfully the way of God. You don't care what anyone thinks nor do you show partiality. [17] Tell us, then, what you think. Is it lawful to pay taxes to Caesar or not?"

[18] Perceiving their malicious intent, Jesus said, "Why are you testing me, hypocrites? [19] Show me the coin used for the tax." They brought him a denarius. [20] "Whose image and inscription is this?" he asked them.

[21] "Caesar's," they said to him.

HERODIANS

Jews who supported Herod the Great's descendants serving as rulers over the land.

Joined with Pharisees in a plot to kill Jesus

Tried to trick Jesus into saying people shouldn't pay taxes

continued

OLD CITY OF JERUSALEM, ISRAEL

Then he said to them, "Give, then, to Caesar the things that are Caesar's, and to God the things that are God's." ²² When they heard this, they were amazed. So they left him and went away.

The Sadducees and the Resurrection

²³ That same day some **Sadducees**, who say there is no resurrection, came up to him and questioned him: ²⁴ "Teacher, Moses said, if a man dies, having no children, his brother is to marry his wife and raise up offspring for his brother. ²⁵ Now there were seven brothers among us. The first got married and died. Having no offspring, he left his wife to his brother. ²⁶ The same thing happened to the second also, and the third, and so on to all seven. ²⁷ Last of all, the woman died. ²⁸ In the resurrection, then, whose wife will she be of the seven? For they all had married her."

²⁹ Jesus answered them, "You are mistaken, because you don't know the Scriptures or the power of God. ³⁰ For in the resurrection they neither marry nor are given in marriage but are like angels in heaven. ³¹ Now concerning the resurrection of the dead, haven't you read what was spoken to you by God: ³² I am the God of Abraham and the God of Isaac and the God of Jacob? He is not the God of the dead, but of the living."

³³ And when the crowds heard this, they were astonished at his teaching.

The Primary Commands

³⁴ When the Pharisees heard that he had silenced the Sadducees, they came together. ³⁵ And one of them, an expert in the law, asked a question to test him: ³⁶ "Teacher, which command in the law is the greatest?"

³⁷ He said to him, "Love the Lord your God with all your heart, with all your soul, and with all your mind. ³⁸ This is the greatest and most important command. ³⁹ The second is like it: Love your neighbor as yourself. ⁴⁰ All the Law and the Prophets depend on these two commands."

SADDUCEES

Politically oriented and focused on maintaining the beliefs and practices of the past

Responsible for the temple and its services

Did not believe in the resurrection of the dead and denied the existence of demons and angels

The Question about the Christ

⁴¹ While the Pharisees were together, Jesus questioned them, ⁴² "What do you think about the Messiah? Whose son is he?"

They replied, "David's."

⁴³ He asked them, "How is it then that David, inspired by the Spirit, calls him 'Lord':

⁴⁴ The Lord declared to my Lord,
'Sit at my right hand
until I put your enemies under your feet'?

⁴⁵ "If David calls him 'Lord,' how then can he be his son?" ⁴⁶ No one was able to answer him at all, and from that day no one dared to question him anymore.

PSALM 110

The Priestly King
A psalm of David.

¹ This is the declaration of the LORD
to my Lord:
"Sit at my right hand
until I make your enemies your footstool."
² The LORD will extend your mighty scepter from Zion.
Rule over your surrounding enemies.
³ Your people will volunteer
on your day of battle.
In holy splendor, from the womb of the dawn,
the dew of your youth belongs to you.
⁴ The LORD has sworn an oath and will not take it back:
"You are a priest forever
according to the pattern of Melchizedek."

⁵ The Lord is at your right hand;
he will crush kings on the day of his anger.
⁶ He will judge the nations, heaping up corpses;
he will crush leaders over the entire world.
⁷ He will drink from the brook by the road;
therefore, he will lift up his head.

HEBREWS 10:11–14

[11] Every priest stands day after day ministering and offering the same sacrifices time after time, which can never take away sins. [12] But this man, after offering one sacrifice for sins forever, sat down at the right hand of God. [13] He is now waiting until his enemies are made his footstool. [14] For by one offering he has perfected forever those who are sanctified.

OBSERVE   *What is happening in the text?*

REFLECT   *What does it teach me about Jesus?*

APPLY   *What is my response?*

Day 23: Jesus Judges the World

Religious Hypocrites Denounced

[1] Then Jesus spoke to the crowds and to his disciples: [2] "The scribes and the Pharisees are seated in the chair of Moses. [3] Therefore do whatever they tell you, and observe it. But don't do what they do, because they don't practice what they teach. [4] They tie up heavy loads that are hard to carry and put them on people's shoulders, but they themselves aren't willing to lift a finger to move them. [5] They do everything to be seen by others: They enlarge their phylacteries and lengthen their tassels. [6] They love the place of honor at banquets, the front seats in the synagogues, [7] greetings in the marketplaces, and to be called 'Rabbi' by people.

[8] "But you are not to be called 'Rabbi,' because you have one Teacher, and you are all brothers and sisters. [9] Do not call anyone on earth your father, because you have one Father, who is in heaven. [10] You are not to be called instructors either, because you have one Instructor, the Messiah. [11] The greatest among you will be your servant. [12] Whoever exalts himself will be humbled, and whoever humbles himself will be exalted.

[13] "Woe to you, scribes and Pharisees, hypocrites! You shut the door of the kingdom of heaven in people's faces. For you don't go in, and you don't allow those entering to go in.

[15] "Woe to you, scribes and Pharisees, hypocrites! You travel over land and sea to make one convert, and when he becomes one, you make him twice as fit for hell as you are!

[16] "Woe to you, blind guides, who say, 'Whoever takes an oath by the temple, it means nothing. But whoever takes an oath by the gold of the temple is bound by his oath.' [17] Blind fools! For which is greater, the gold or the temple that sanctified the gold? [18] Also, 'Whoever takes an oath by the altar, it means nothing; but whoever takes an oath by the gift that is on it is bound by his oath.' [19] Blind people! For which is greater, the gift or the altar that sanctifies the gift? [20] Therefore, the one who takes an oath by the altar takes an oath by it and by everything on it. [21] The one who takes an oath by the temple takes an oath by it and by him who dwells in it. [22] And the one who takes an oath by heaven takes an oath by God's throne and by him who sits on it.

[23] "Woe to you, scribes and Pharisees, hypocrites! You pay a tenth of mint, dill, and cumin, and yet you have neglected the more important matters of the law—justice, mercy, and faithfulness. These things should have been done without neglecting the others. [24] Blind guides! You strain out a gnat, but gulp down a camel!

continued

THE WESTERN WALL, JERUSALEM, ISRAEL

25 "Woe to you, scribes and Pharisees, hypocrites! You clean the outside of the cup and dish, but inside they are full of greed and self-indulgence. 26 Blind Pharisee! First clean the inside of the cup, so that the outside of it may also become clean.

27 "Woe to you, scribes and Pharisees, hypocrites! You are like whitewashed tombs, which appear beautiful on the outside, but inside are full of the bones of the dead and every kind of impurity. 28 In the same way, on the outside you seem righteous to people, but inside you are full of hypocrisy and lawlessness.

29 "Woe to you, scribes and Pharisees, hypocrites! You build the tombs of the prophets and decorate the graves of the righteous, 30 and you say, 'If we had lived in the days of our ancestors, we wouldn't have taken part with them in shedding the prophets' blood.' 31 So you testify against yourselves that you are descendants of those who murdered the prophets. 32 Fill up, then, the measure of your ancestors' sins!

33 "Snakes! Brood of vipers! How can you escape being condemned to hell? 34 This is why I am sending you prophets, sages, and scribes. Some of them you will kill and crucify, and some of them you will flog in your synagogues and pursue from town to town. 35 So all the righteous blood shed on the earth will be charged to you, from the blood of righteous Abel to the blood of Zechariah, son of Berechiah, whom you murdered between the sanctuary and the altar. 36 Truly I tell you, all these things will come on this generation.

Jesus's Lamenting over Jerusalem

37 "Jerusalem, Jerusalem, who kills the prophets and stones those who are sent to her. How often I wanted to gather your children together, as a hen gathers her chicks under her wings, but you were not willing! 38 See, your house is left to you desolate. 39 For I tell you, you will not see me again until you say, 'Blessed is he who comes in the name of the Lord'!"

EXODUS 10:21-23

The Ninth Plague: Darkness

21 Then the LORD said to Moses, "Stretch out your hand toward heaven, and there will be darkness over the land of Egypt, a darkness that can be felt." 22 So Moses stretched out his hand toward heaven, and there was thick darkness throughout the land of Egypt for three days. 23 One person could not see another, and for three days they did not move from where they were. Yet all the Israelites had light where they lived.

ROMANS 8:22-23

22 For we know that the whole creation has been groaning together with labor pains until now. 23 Not only that, but we ourselves who have the Spirit as the firstfruits—we also groan within ourselves, eagerly waiting for adoption, the redemption of our bodies.

OBSERVE   *What is happening in the text?*

REFLECT   *What does it teach me about Jesus?*

APPLY   *What is my response?*

Day 24:
Jesus Will
Come Again

MATTHEW 24

Destruction of the Temple Predicted

¹ As Jesus left and was going out of the temple, his disciples came up and called his attention to its buildings. ² He replied to them, "Do you see all these things? Truly I tell you, not one stone will be left here on another that will not be thrown down."

Signs of the End of the Age

³ While he was sitting on the Mount of Olives, the disciples approached him privately and said, "Tell us, when will these things happen? And what is the sign of your coming and of the end of the age?"

⁴ Jesus replied to them: "Watch out that no one deceives you. ⁵ For many will come in my name, saying, 'I am the Messiah,' and they will deceive many. ⁶ You are going to hear of wars and rumors of wars. See that you are not alarmed, because these things must take place, but the end is not yet. ⁷ For nation will rise up against nation, and kingdom against kingdom. There will be famines and earthquakes in various places. ⁸ All these events are the beginning of labor pains.

Persecutions Predicted

⁹ "Then they will hand you over to be persecuted, and they will kill you. You will be hated by all nations because of my name. ¹⁰ Then many will fall away, betray one another, and hate one another. ¹¹ Many false prophets will rise up and deceive many. ¹² Because lawlessness will multiply, the love of many will grow cold. ¹³ But the one who endures to the end will be saved. ¹⁴ This good news of the kingdom will be proclaimed in all the world as a testimony to all nations, and then the end will come.

The Great Tribulation

¹⁵ "So when you see the abomination of desolation, spoken of by the prophet Daniel, standing in the holy place" (let the reader understand), ¹⁶ "then those in Judea must flee to the mountains. ¹⁷ A man on the housetop must not come down to get things out of his house, ¹⁸ and a man in the field must not go back to get his coat. ¹⁹ Woe to pregnant women and nursing mothers in those days! ²⁰ Pray that your escape may not be in winter or on a Sabbath. ²¹ For at that time there will be great distress, the kind that hasn't taken place from the beginning of the world until now and never will again. ²² Unless those days were cut short, no one would be saved. But those days will be cut short because of the elect.

²³ "If anyone tells you then, 'See, here is the Messiah!' or, 'Over here!' do not believe it. ²⁴ For false messiahs and false prophets will arise and perform great signs and wonders to lead astray, if possible, even the elect. ²⁵ Take note: I have told you in advance. ²⁶ So if they tell you, 'See, he's in the wilderness!' don't go out; or, 'See, he's in the storerooms!' do not believe it. ²⁷ For as the lightning comes from the east and flashes as far as the west, so will be the coming of the Son of Man. ²⁸ Wherever the carcass is, there the vultures will gather.

NEGEV

"Heaven and earth will pass away, but my words will never pass away."

24:35

The Coming of the Son of Man

29 "Immediately after the distress of those days, the sun will be darkened, and the moon will not shed its light; the stars will fall from the sky, and the powers of the heavens will be shaken. 30 Then the sign of the Son of Man will appear in the sky, and then all the peoples of the earth will mourn; and they will see the Son of Man coming on the clouds of heaven with power and great glory. 31 He will send out his angels with a loud trumpet, and they will gather his elect from the four winds, from one end of the sky to the other.

The Parable of the Fig Tree

32 "Learn this lesson from the fig tree: As soon as its branch becomes tender and sprouts leaves, you know that summer is near. 33 In the same way, when you see all these things, recognize that he is near—at the door. 34 Truly I tell you, this generation will certainly not pass away until all these things take place. 35 Heaven and earth will pass away, but my words will never pass away.

No One Knows the Day or Hour

36 "Now concerning that day and hour no one knows—neither the angels of heaven nor the Son—except the Father alone. 37 As the days of Noah were, so the coming of the Son of Man will be. 38 For in those days before the flood they were eating and drinking, marrying and giving in marriage, until the day Noah boarded the ark. 39 They didn't know until the flood came and swept them all away. This is the way the coming of the Son of Man will be. 40 Then two men will be in the field; one will be taken and one left. 41 Two women will be grinding grain with a hand mill; one will be taken and one left. 42 Therefore be alert, since you don't know what day your Lord is coming. 43 But know this: If the homeowner had known what time the thief was coming, he would have stayed alert and not let his house be broken into. 44 This is why you are also to be ready, because the Son of Man is coming at an hour you do not expect.

Faithful Service to Christ

45 "Who then is a faithful and wise servant, whom his master has put in charge of his household, to give them food at the proper time? 46 Blessed is that servant whom the master finds doing his job when he comes. 47 Truly I tell you, he will put him in charge of all his possessions. 48 But if that wicked servant says in his heart, 'My master is delayed,' 49 and starts to beat his fellow servants, and eats and drinks with drunkards, 50 that servant's master will come on a day he does not expect him and at an hour he does not know. 51 He will cut him to pieces and assign him a place with the hypocrites, where there will be weeping and gnashing of teeth."

The Parable of the Ten Virgins

[1] "At that time the kingdom of heaven will be like ten virgins who took their lamps and went out to meet the groom. [2] Five of them were foolish and five were wise. [3] When the foolish took their lamps, they didn't take oil with them; [4] but the wise ones took oil in their flasks with their lamps. [5] When the groom was delayed, they all became drowsy and fell asleep.

[6] "In the middle of the night there was a shout: 'Here's the groom! Come out to meet him.'

[7] "Then all the virgins got up and trimmed their lamps. [8] The foolish ones said to the wise ones, 'Give us some of your oil, because our lamps are going out.'

[9] "The wise ones answered, 'No, there won't be enough for us and for you. Go instead to those who sell oil, and buy some for yourselves.'

[10] "When they had gone to buy some, the groom arrived, and those who were ready went in with him to the wedding banquet, and the door was shut. [11] Later the rest of the virgins also came and said, 'Master, master, open up for us!'

[12] "He replied, 'Truly I tell you, I don't know you!'

[13] "Therefore be alert, because you don't know either the day or the hour.

The Parable of the Talents

[14] "For it is just like a man about to go on a journey. He called his own servants and entrusted his possessions to them. [15] To one he gave five talents, to another two talents, and to another one talent, depending on each one's ability. Then he went on a journey. Immediately [16] the man who had received five talents went, put them to work, and earned five more. [17] In the same way the man with two earned two more. [18] But the man who had received one talent went off, dug a hole in the ground, and hid his master's money.

[19] "After a long time the master of those servants came and settled accounts with them. [20] The man who had received five talents approached, presented five more talents, and said, 'Master, you gave me five talents. See, I've earned five more talents.'

[21] "His master said to him, 'Well done, good and faithful servant! You were faithful over a few things; I will put you in charge of many things. Share your master's joy.'

[22] "The man with two talents also approached. He said, 'Master, you gave me two talents. See, I've earned two more talents.'

[23] "His master said to him, 'Well done, good and faithful servant! You were faithful over a few things; I will put you in charge of many things. Share your master's joy.'

[24] "The man who had received one talent also approached and said, 'Master, I know you. You're a harsh man, reaping where you haven't sown and gathering where you haven't scattered seed. [25] So I was afraid and went off and hid your talent in the ground. See, you have what is yours.'

[26] "His master replied to him, 'You evil, lazy servant! If you knew that I reap where I haven't sown and gather where I haven't scattered, [27] then you should have deposited my money with the bankers, and I would have received my money back with interest when I returned.

[28] "'So take the talent from him and give it to the one who has ten talents. [29] For to everyone who has, more will be given, and he will have more than enough. But from the one who does not have, even what he has will be taken away from him. [30] And throw this good-for-nothing servant into the outer darkness, where there will be weeping and gnashing of teeth.'

The Sheep and the Goats

[31] "When the Son of Man comes in his glory, and all the angels with him, then he will sit on his glorious throne. [32] All the nations will be gathered before him, and he will separate them one from another, just as a shepherd separates the sheep from the goats. [33] He will put the sheep on his right and the goats on the left. [34] Then the King will say

to those on his right, 'Come, you who are blessed by my Father; inherit the kingdom prepared for you from the foundation of the world.

35 "'For I was hungry and you gave me something to eat; I was thirsty and you gave me something to drink; I was a stranger and you took me in; 36 I was naked and you clothed me; I was sick and you took care of me; I was in prison and you visited me.'

37 "Then the righteous will answer him, 'Lord, when did we see you hungry and feed you, or thirsty and give you something to drink? 38 When did we see you a stranger and take you in, or without clothes and clothe you? 39 When did we see you sick, or in prison, and visit you?'

40 "And the King will answer them, 'Truly I tell you, whatever you did for one of the least of these brothers and sisters of mine, you did for me.'

41 "Then he will also say to those on the left, 'Depart from me, you who are cursed, into the eternal fire prepared for the devil and his angels! 42 For I was hungry and you gave me nothing to eat; I was thirsty and you gave me nothing to drink; 43 I was a stranger and you didn't take me in; I was naked and you didn't clothe me, sick and in prison and you didn't take care of me.'

44 "Then they too will answer, 'Lord, when did we see you hungry, or thirsty, or a stranger, or without clothes, or sick, or in prison, and not help you?'

45 "Then he will answer them, 'I tell you, whatever you did not do for one of the least of these, you did not do for me.'

46 "And they will go away into eternal punishment, but the righteous into eternal life."

DANIEL 7:13-14

13 I continued watching in the night visions,

and suddenly one like a son of man
was coming with the clouds of heaven.
He approached the Ancient of Days
and was escorted before him.
14 He was given dominion,
and glory, and a kingdom;
so that those of every people,
nation, and language
should serve him.
His dominion is an everlasting dominion
that will not pass away,
and his kingdom is one
that will not be destroyed.

OBSERVE   *What is happening in the text?*

REFLECT   *What does it teach me about Jesus?*

APPLY   *What is my response?*

Day 25:
Jesus Gives
His Life

The Plot to Kill Jesus

[1] When Jesus had finished saying all these things, he told his disciples, [2] "You know that the Passover takes place after two days, and the Son of Man will be handed over to be crucified."

[3] Then the chief priests and the elders of the people assembled in the courtyard of the high priest, who was named **Caiaphas**, [4] and they conspired to arrest Jesus in a treacherous way and kill him. [5] "Not during the festival," they said, "so there won't be rioting among the people."

The Anointing at Bethany

[6] While Jesus was in Bethany at the house of **Simon the leper**, [7] a woman approached him with an alabaster jar of very expensive perfume. She poured it on his head as he was reclining at the table. [8] When the disciples saw it, they were indignant. "Why this waste?" they asked. [9] "This might have been sold for a great deal and given to the poor."

[10] Aware of this, Jesus said to them, "Why are you bothering this woman? She has done a noble thing for me. [11] You always have the poor with you, but you do not always have me. [12] By pouring this perfume on my body, she has prepared me for burial. [13] Truly I tell you, wherever this gospel is proclaimed in the whole world, what she has done will also be told in memory of her."

[14] Then one of the Twelve, the man called Judas Iscariot, went to the chief priests [15] and said, "What are you willing to give me if I hand him over to you?" So they weighed out thirty pieces of silver for him. [16] And from that time he started looking for a good opportunity to betray him.

Betrayal at the Passover

[17] On the first day of Unleavened Bread the disciples came to Jesus and asked, "Where do you want us to make preparations for you to eat the Passover?"

[18] "Go into the city to a certain man," he said, "and tell him, 'The Teacher says: My time is near; I am celebrating the Passover at your place with my disciples.'" [19] So the disciples did as Jesus had directed them and prepared the Passover. [20] When evening came, he was reclining at the table with the Twelve. [21] While they were eating, he said, "Truly I tell you, one of you will betray me."

[22] Deeply distressed, each one began to say to him, "Surely not I, Lord?"

[23] He replied, "The one who dipped his hand with me in the bowl—he will betray me. [24] The Son of Man will go just as it is written about him, but woe to that man by whom the Son of Man is betrayed! It would have been better for him if he had not been born."

[25] Judas, his betrayer, replied, "Surely not I, Rabbi?"

"You have said it," he told him.

The First Lord's Supper

²⁶ As they were eating, Jesus took bread, blessed and broke it, gave it to the disciples, and said, "Take and eat it; this is my body." ²⁷ Then he took a cup, and after giving thanks, he gave it to them and said, "Drink from it, all of you. ²⁸ For this is my blood of the covenant, which is poured out for many for the forgiveness of sins. ²⁹ But I tell you, I will not drink from this fruit of the vine from now on until that day when I drink it new with you in my Father's kingdom." ³⁰ After singing a hymn, they went out to the Mount of Olives.

Peter's Denial Predicted

³¹ Then Jesus said to them, "Tonight all of you will fall away because of me, for it is written:

> I will strike the shepherd,
> and the sheep of the flock will be
> scattered.

³² But after I have risen, I will go ahead of you to Galilee."

³³ Peter told him, "Even if everyone falls away because of you, I will never fall away."

³⁴ "Truly I tell you," Jesus said to him, "tonight, before the rooster crows, you will deny me three times."

³⁵ "Even if I have to die with you," Peter told him, "I will never deny you," and all the disciples said the same thing.

OLD CITY OF JERUSALEM, ISRAEL

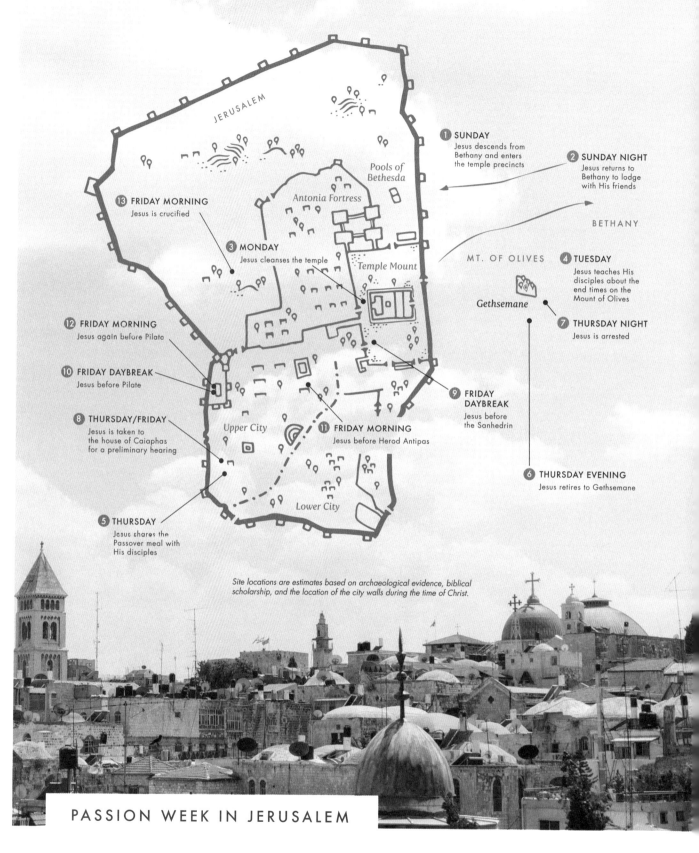

JERUSALEM

Pools of Bethesda

Antonia Fortress

Temple Mount

1 SUNDAY
Jesus descends from Bethany and enters the temple precincts

2 SUNDAY NIGHT
Jesus returns to Bethany to lodge with His friends

BETHANY

MT. OF OLIVES

4 TUESDAY
Jesus teaches His disciples about the end times on the Mount of Olives

Gethsemane

7 THURSDAY NIGHT
Jesus is arrested

13 FRIDAY MORNING
Jesus is crucified

3 MONDAY
Jesus cleanses the temple

12 FRIDAY MORNING
Jesus again before Pilate

10 FRIDAY DAYBREAK
Jesus before Pilate

9 FRIDAY DAYBREAK
Jesus before the Sanhedrin

8 THURSDAY/FRIDAY
Jesus is taken to the house of Caiaphas for a preliminary hearing

Upper City

11 FRIDAY MORNING
Jesus before Herod Antipas

6 THURSDAY EVENING
Jesus retires to Gethsemane

5 THURSDAY
Jesus shares the Passover meal with His disciples

Lower City

Site locations are estimates based on archaeological evidence, biblical scholarship, and the location of the city walls during the time of Christ.

PASSION WEEK IN JERUSALEM

The Prayer in the Garden

36 Then Jesus came with them to a place called Gethsemane, and he told the disciples, "Sit here while I go over there and pray." 37 Taking along Peter and the two sons of Zebedee, he began to be sorrowful and troubled. 38 He said to them, "I am deeply grieved to the point of death. Remain here and stay awake with me." 39 Going a little farther, he fell facedown and prayed, "My Father, if it is possible, let this cup pass from me. Yet not as I will, but as you will."

40 Then he came to the disciples and found them sleeping. He asked Peter, "So, couldn't you stay awake with me one hour? 41 Stay awake and pray, so that you won't enter into temptation. The spirit is willing, but the flesh is weak."

42 Again, a second time, he went away and prayed, "My Father, if this cannot pass unless I drink it, your will be done." 43 And he came again and found them sleeping, because they could not keep their eyes open.

44 After leaving them, he went away again and prayed a third time, saying the same thing once more. 45 Then he came to the disciples and said to them, "Are you still sleeping and resting? See, the time is near. The Son of Man is betrayed into the hands of sinners. 46 Get up; let's go. See, my betrayer is near."

Judas's Betrayal of Jesus

47 While he was still speaking, Judas, one of the Twelve, suddenly arrived. A large mob with swords and clubs was with him from the chief priests and elders of the people. 48 His betrayer had given them a sign: "The one I kiss, he's the one; arrest him." 49 So immediately he went up to Jesus and said, "Greetings, Rabbi!" and kissed him.

50 "Friend," Jesus asked him, "why have you come?"

Then they came up, took hold of Jesus, and arrested him. 51 At that moment one of those with Jesus reached out his hand and drew his sword. He struck the high priest's servant and cut off his ear.

52 Then Jesus told him, "Put your sword back in its place because all who take up the sword will perish by the sword. 53 Or do you think that I cannot call on my Father, and he will provide me here and now with more than twelve legions of angels? 54 How, then, would the Scriptures be fulfilled that say it must happen this way?"

55 At that time Jesus said to the crowds, "Have you come out with swords and clubs, as if I were a criminal, to capture me? Every day I used to sit, teaching in the temple, and you didn't arrest me. 56 But all this has happened so that the writings of the prophets would be fulfilled." Then all the disciples deserted him and ran away.

Jesus Faces the Sanhedrin

57 Those who had arrested Jesus led him away to Caiaphas the high priest, where the scribes and the elders had convened. 58 Peter was following him at a distance right to the high priest's courtyard. He went in and was sitting with the servants to see the outcome.

59 The chief priests and the whole **Sanhedrin** were looking for false testimony against Jesus so that they could put him to death, 60 but they could not find any, even though many false witnesses came forward. Finally, two who came forward 61 stated, "This man said, 'I can destroy the temple of God and rebuild it in three days.'"

THE SANHEDRIN

A seventy-one-member Jewish council in Jerusalem run by the high priest

Made up of Sadducees, Pharisees, priests, and elders of the people

Had local authority over the Jewish community under Roman oversight

62 The high priest stood up and said to him, "Don't you have an answer to what these men are testifying against you?" 63 But Jesus kept silent. The high priest said to him, "I charge you under oath by the living God: Tell us if you are the Messiah, the Son of God."

64 "You have said it," Jesus told him. "But I tell you, in the future you will see the Son of Man seated at the right hand of Power and coming on the clouds of heaven."

65 Then the high priest tore his robes and said, "He has blasphemed! Why do we still need witnesses? See, now you've heard the blasphemy. 66 What is your decision?"

They answered, "He deserves death!" 67 Then they spat in his face and beat him; others slapped him 68 and said, "Prophesy to us, Messiah! Who was it that hit you?"

Peter Denies His Lord

⁶⁹ Now Peter was sitting outside in the courtyard. A servant girl approached him and said, "You were with Jesus the Galilean too."

⁷⁰ But he denied it in front of everyone: "I don't know what you're talking about."

⁷¹ When he had gone out to the gateway, another woman saw him and told those who were there, "This man was with Jesus the Nazarene!"

⁷² And again he denied it with an oath: "I don't know the man!"

⁷³ After a little while those standing there approached and said to Peter, "You really are one of them, since even your accent gives you away."

⁷⁴ Then he started to curse and to swear with an oath, "I don't know the man!" Immediately a rooster crowed, ⁷⁵ and Peter remembered the words Jesus had spoken, "Before the rooster crows, you will deny me three times." And he went outside and wept bitterly.

LEVITICUS 23:5-6

⁵ The Passover to the LORD comes in the first month, at twilight on the fourteenth day of the month. ⁶ The Festival of Unleavened Bread to the LORD is on the fifteenth day of the same month. For seven days you must eat unleavened bread.

ISAIAH 53:7

He was oppressed and afflicted,
yet he did not open his mouth.
Like a lamb led to the slaughter
and like a sheep silent before her shearers,
he did not open his mouth.

JEREMIAH 31:31

"Look, the days are coming"—this is the LORD's declaration—"when I will make a new covenant with the house of Israel and with the house of Judah."

OBSERVE   *What is happening in the text?*

REFLECT   *What does it teach me about Jesus?*

APPLY   *What is my response?*

Day 26:
Jesus Is
Risen

MATTHEW 27

Jesus Handed Over to Pilate

[1] When daybreak came, all the chief priests and the elders of the people plotted against Jesus to put him to death. [2] After tying him up, they led him away and handed him over to **Pilate**, the governor.

Judas Hangs Himself

[3] Then Judas, his betrayer, seeing that Jesus had been condemned, was full of remorse and returned the thirty pieces of silver to the chief priests and elders. [4] "I have sinned by betraying innocent blood," he said.

"What's that to us?" they said. "See to it yourself!" [5] So he threw the silver into the temple and departed. Then he went and hanged himself.

[6] The chief priests took the silver and said, "It's not permitted to put it into the temple treasury, since it is blood money." [7] They conferred together and bought the potter's field with it as a burial place for foreigners. [8] Therefore that field has been called "Blood Field" to this day. [9] Then what was spoken through the prophet Jeremiah was fulfilled: They took the thirty pieces of silver, the price of him whose price was set by the Israelites, [10] and they gave them for the potter's field, as the Lord directed me.

Jesus Faces the Governor

[11] Now Jesus stood before the governor. "Are you the King of the **Jews**?" the governor asked him.

Jesus answered, "You say so." [12] While he was being accused by the chief priests and elders, he didn't answer.

[13] Then Pilate said to him, "Don't you hear how much they are testifying against you?" [14] But he didn't answer him on even one charge, so that the governor was quite amazed.

JEWS

From Judea
and Galilee

Descendants of
Abraham

Believers in one
God: the God of
Abraham, Isaac,
and Jacob

Jesus or Barabbas

[15] At the festival the governor's custom was to release to the crowd a prisoner they wanted. [16] At that time they had a notorious prisoner called Barabbas. [17] So when they had gathered together, Pilate said to them, "Who is it you want me to release for you—**Barabbas**, or Jesus who is called Christ?" [18] For he knew it was because of envy that they had handed him over.

[19] While he was sitting on the judge's bench, his wife sent word to him, "Have nothing to do with that righteous man, for today I've suffered terribly in a dream because of him."

SHEPHERDS' FIELDS IN BETHLEHEM

20 The chief priests and the elders, however, persuaded the crowds to ask for Barabbas and to execute Jesus. 21 The governor asked them, "Which of the two do you want me to release for you?"

"Barabbas!" they answered.

22 Pilate asked them, "What should I do then with Jesus, who is called Christ?"

They all answered, "Crucify him!"

23 Then he said, "Why? What has he done wrong?"

But they kept shouting all the more, "Crucify him!"

24 When Pilate saw that he was getting nowhere, but that a riot was starting instead, he took some water, washed his hands in front of the crowd, and said, "I am innocent of this man's blood. See to it yourselves!"

25 All the people answered, "His blood be on us and on our children!" 26 Then he released Barabbas to them and, after having Jesus flogged, handed him over to be crucified.

Mocked by the Military

27 Then the governor's soldiers took Jesus into the governor's residence and gathered the whole company around him. 28 They stripped him and dressed him in a scarlet robe. 29 They twisted together a crown of thorns, put it on his head, and placed a staff in his right hand. And they knelt down before him and mocked him· "Hail, King of the Jews!" 30 Then they spat on him, took the staff, and kept hitting him on the head. 31 After they had mocked him, they stripped him of the robe, put his own clothes on him, and led him away to crucify him.

Crucified Between Two Criminals

32 As they were going out, they found a **Cyrenian man named Simon.** They forced him to carry his cross. 33 When they came to a place called Golgotha (which means Place of the Skull), 34 they gave him wine mixed with gall to drink. But when he tasted it, he refused to drink it. 35 After crucifying him, they divided his clothes by casting lots. 36 Then they sat down and were guarding him there. 37 Above his head they put up the charge against him in writing: This Is Jesus, the King of the Jews.

38 Then two criminals were crucified with him, one on the right and one on the left. 39 Those who passed by were yelling insults at him, shaking their heads 40 and saying, "You who would destroy the temple and rebuild it in three days, save yourself! If you are the Son of God, come down from the cross!" 41 In the same way the chief priests, with the scribes and elders, mocked him and said, 42 "He saved others, but he cannot save himself! He is the King of Israel! Let him come down now from the cross, and we will believe in him. 43 He trusts in God; let God rescue him now—if he takes pleasure in him! For he said, 'I am the Son of God.'" 44 In the same way even the criminals who were crucified with him taunted him.

The Death of Jesus

45 From noon until three in the afternoon darkness came over the whole land. 46 About three in the afternoon Jesus cried out with a loud voice, *"Elí, Elí, lemá sabachtháni?"* that is, "My God, my God, why have you abandoned me?"

47 When some of those standing there heard this, they said, "He's calling for Elijah."

48 Immediately one of them ran and got a sponge, filled it with sour wine, put it on a stick, and offered him a drink. 49 But the rest said, "Let's see if Elijah comes to save him."

50 But Jesus cried out again with a loud voice and gave up his spirit. 51 Suddenly, the curtain of the sanctuary was torn in two from top to bottom, the earth quaked, and the rocks were split. 52 The tombs were also opened and many bodies of the saints who had fallen asleep were raised. 53 And they came out of the tombs after his resurrection, entered the holy city, and appeared to many.

54 When the centurion and those with him, who were keeping watch over Jesus, saw the earthquake and the things that had happened, they were terrified and said, "Truly this man was the Son of God!"

55 Many women who had followed Jesus from Galilee and looked after him were there, watching from a distance. 56 Among them were **Mary Magdalene, Mary the mother of James and Joseph,** and the mother of Zebedee's sons.

EIN GEDI, ISRAEL

The Burial of Jesus

⁵⁷ When it was evening, **a rich man from Arimathea named Joseph** came, who himself had also become a disciple of Jesus. ⁵⁸ He approached Pilate and asked for Jesus's body. Then Pilate ordered that it be released. ⁵⁹ So Joseph took the body, wrapped it in clean, fine linen, ⁶⁰ and placed it in his new tomb, which he had cut into the rock. He left after rolling a great stone against the entrance of the tomb. ⁶¹ Mary Magdalene and the other Mary were seated there, facing the tomb.

The Closely Guarded Tomb

⁶² The next day, which followed the preparation day, the chief priests and the Pharisees gathered before Pilate ⁶³ and said, "Sir, we remember that while this deceiver was still alive he said, 'After three days I will rise again.' ⁶⁴ So give orders that the tomb be made secure until the third day. Otherwise, his disciples may come, steal him, and tell the people, 'He has been raised from the dead,' and the last deception will be worse than the first."

⁶⁵ "You have a guard of soldiers," Pilate told them. "Go and make it as secure as you know how." ⁶⁶ They went and secured the tomb by setting a seal on the stone and placing the guard.

"He is not here. For he has risen, just as he said." 28:6

Resurrection Morning

[1] After the Sabbath, as the first day of the week was dawning, Mary Magdalene and the other Mary went to view the tomb. [2] There was a violent earthquake, because an angel of the Lord descended from heaven and approached the tomb. He rolled back the stone and was sitting on it. [3] His appearance was like lightning, and his clothing was as white as snow. [4] The guards were so shaken by fear of him that they became like dead men.

[5] The angel told the women, "Don't be afraid, because I know you are looking for Jesus who was crucified. [6] He is not here. For he has risen, just as he said. Come and see the place where he lay. [7] Then go quickly and tell his disciples, 'He has risen from the dead and indeed he is going ahead of you to Galilee; you will see him there.' Listen, I have told you."

[8] So, departing quickly from the tomb with fear and great joy, they ran to tell his disciples the news. [9] Just then Jesus met them and said, "Greetings!" They came up, took hold of his feet, and worshiped him. [10] Then Jesus told them, "Do not be afraid. Go and tell my brothers to leave for Galilee, and they will see me there."

The Soldiers Bribed to Lie

[11] As they were on their way, some of the guards came into the city and reported to the chief priests everything that had happened. [12] After the priests had assembled with the elders and agreed on a plan, they gave the soldiers a large sum of money [13] and told them, "Say this, 'His disciples came during the night and stole him while we were sleeping.' [14] If this reaches the governor's ears, we will deal with him and keep you out of trouble." [15] They took the money and did as they were instructed, and this story has been spread among Jewish people to this day.

The Great Commission

[16] The eleven disciples traveled to Galilee, to the mountain where Jesus had directed them. [17] When they saw him, they worshiped, but some doubted. [18] Jesus came near and said to them, "All authority has been given to me in heaven and on earth. [19] Go, therefore, and make disciples of all nations, baptizing them in the name of the Father and of the Son and of the Holy Spirit, [20] teaching them to observe everything I have commanded you. And remember, I am with you always, to the end of the age."

PSALM 22:7-8

[7] Everyone who sees me mocks me;
they sneer and shake their heads:
[8] "He relies on the LORD;
let him save him;
let the LORD rescue him,
since he takes pleasure in him."

1 CORINTHIANS 15:6

Then he appeared to over five hundred brothers and sisters at one time; most of them are still alive, but some have fallen asleep.

2 CORINTHIANS 3:18

We all, with unveiled faces, are looking as in a mirror at the glory of the Lord and are being transformed into the same image from glory to glory; this is from the Lord who is the Spirit.

OBSERVE   *What is happening in the text?*

REFLECT   *What does it teach me about Jesus?*

APPLY   *What is my response?*

Who Is Jesus?

KEY CHARACTERIS-
TICS OF CHRIST IN
THE GOSPELS

I   *Jesus is the Son of God.*
Through the authors, the disciples, the Gentiles, and Jesus Himself,
all four Gospels testify that Christ is the Son of God.

2   *Jesus is God who became human.*
Jesus is both fully God and fully man. The deity and humanity of
Jesus are displayed through the testimony of the Gospel writers and
the disciples.

3   *Jesus is the Christ, the Messiah.*
Jesus is the Messiah, the promised deliverer of the nation of Israel
and of all humanity.

4   *Jesus came to save sinners.*
Jesus's purpose on earth was to save sinners by taking their
punishment on Himself.

5   *Jesus has power to forgive sins.*
Because He is God, Jesus has the authority to forgive sins.

6   *Jesus has authority over death.*
Jesus has power to raise the dead. He conquered death through
His perfect life, sacrificial death, and glorious resurrection.

7   *Jesus has power to give eternal life.*
God has given Jesus authority to grant eternal life to all those who
believe in Him.

8   *Jesus healed the sick.*
Jesus has power over all physical sickness. While on earth, He
healed many people, from those with skin diseases and fevers to
those blind and lame from birth.

9   *Jesus taught with authority.*
As the Son of God, Jesus has authority over heaven and earth.

IO   *Jesus is compassionate.*
Jesus showed compassion for all people—those who were lost and
those who followed Him.

II   *Jesus experienced sorrow.*
Jesus experienced sorrow and many other emotions.

I2   *Jesus never disobeyed God.*
Jesus lived a perfect life without sin. Even though He was tempted,
He modeled how to use Scripture to resist temptation.

MATTHEW	MARK	LUKE	JOHN
16:15–16; 27:54	**1:1**	22:70–71	8:24
2:11	**8:27–30**	9:28-36	1:1–2,14; 20:28
26:63–64	**14:61–62**	9:20	4:25–26
9:13	**2:17**	5:32	12:47
9:1-8	**2:9–12**	24:47	8:2–11
28:5–6	**5:22–24; 35–42**	24:5–6	11:1–44
8:5–13	**9:1**	23:43	10:28; 17:2
8:5–13	**1:32–34**	5:12–15	9:1–17
7:29	**1:21–22**	8:22–25	6:16–21
9:36	**1:41; 8:2**	23:34	5:5–9
26:38	**10:14**	22:44	11:35
4:1–11	**1:12–13**	22:42	8:46

Day 27:
Grace Day

Use this day to pray, rest, and reflect
on this week's reading, giving thanks
for the grace that is ours in Christ.

Daniel 7:14

HE WAS GIVEN DOMINION,
AND GLORY, AND A KINGDOM;
SO THAT THOSE OF EVERY PEOPLE,
NATION, AND LANGUAGE
SHOULD SERVE HIM.
HIS DOMINION IS AN EVERLASTING DOMINION
THAT WILL NOT PASS AWAY,
AND HIS KINGDOM IS ONE
THAT WILL NOT BE DESTROYED.

Day 28:
Weekly Truth

Scripture is God-breathed and true. When we memorize it, we carry the good news of the gospel of Jesus with us wherever we go.

This week's verse captures the heart of why Matthew wrote his Gospel.

Matthew 28:6

He is not here. For he has risen, just as he said. Come and see the place where he lay.

Key People

IN MATTHEW

b

Barabbas

Notorious prisoner whom Pilate released at the crowd's request instead of Jesus (Mt 27:15–26)

c

Caiaphas, the High Priest

High priest in Jerusalem who oversaw Jesus's trial (Mt 26:3)

Son-in-law of Annas, who led the plot to kill Jesus (Jn 18:13–14)

h

Herod Antipas

Youngest son of Herod the Great (Lk 3:1)

Tetrarch (one of four rulers) of Galilee who beheaded John the Baptist (Mt 14:1–12)

Ruled over Galilee during Jesus' trial and crucifixion; questioned Jesus at Pilate's request (Lk 23:6–12)

Herod the Great

King of Judea when Jesus was born (Mt 2:1)

Tried to trick the wise men into revealing Jesus' location (Mt 2:2–8)

Enraged that he could not find Jesus, ordered the execution of all male children under the age of two near Bethlehem (Mt 2:16–18)

j

James, brother of Jesus

The oldest of Jesus's younger half-brothers—Joseph, Simon, and Judas—and half-sisters (Mt 13:55–56)

Became a key leader in the Jerusalem church (Ac 12:17)

Author of the book of James (Jms 1:1)

John the Baptist

Jesus's cousin, son of Elizabeth and Zechariah (Lk 1:57–66)

The promised one who would prepare the way for Jesus (Lk 1:5–17)

Baptized people in the Jordan River, calling all to repent and believe in the Messiah (Mt 3:1–6)

Joseph of Arimathea

Wealthy man who became a secret disciple of Jesus (Jn 19:38)

Anointed Jesus's body with perfume after the crucifixion (Jn 19:39–40)

Buried Jesus's body in a tomb he owned (Mt 27:57–60)

Joseph, son of Jacob

Husband to Mary, earthly father figure to Jesus (Mt 1:18–23)

Present with Mary at Jesus's birth (Lk 2:4–7)

m

Mary, mother of James and Joseph

One of several Marys mentioned in the Gospels; not Jesus's mother; sometimes called "the other Mary" (Mt 27:56, 61)

Disciple of Jesus, present with Mary Magdalene at the empty tomb (Mt 27:55–56; 28:5–7)

Mary, mother of Jesus

The virgin who gave birth to Jesus in Bethlehem (Mt 1:18–2:1)

Mary Magdalene

Had seven demons whom Jesus cast out (Lk 8:2)

Watched Joseph of Arimathea bury Jesus's body (Mt 27:61)

One of the first to see the empty tomb and the risen Jesus (Mt 28:1–7)

Told the disciples Jesus had risen (Mt 28:8–10)

Mother of Zebedee's sons

Possibly Salome (Mk 16:1)

The mother of James and John, asked Jesus to let her sons sit at His right and left hand in glory (Mt 20:20–21)

p

Pontius Pilate

Governor of Judea who sentenced Jesus to be crucified (Mt 27:2, 24–26)

s

Simon of Cyrene

Worshiper in Jerusalem who was forced to carry Jesus's cross for Him (Mt 27:32)

Simon the Leper

Hosted Jesus and His disciples during the week Jesus was crucified (Mt 26:6)

DOWNLOAD THE APP

STOP BY
shereadstruth.com

SHOP
shopshereadstruth.com

SEND A NOTE
hello@shereadstruth.com

CONNECT
#SheReadsTruth

SHE READS TRUTH *is a worldwide community of women who read God's Word together every day.*

Founded in 2012, She Reads Truth invites women of all ages to engage with Scripture through daily reading plans, online conversation led by a vibrant community of contributors, and offline resources created at the intersection of beauty, goodness, and Truth.

WHERE DID I STUDY?

O HOME
O OFFICE
O COFFEE SHOP
O CHURCH
O A FRIEND'S HOUSE
O OTHER

WHAT WAS I LISTENING TO?

ARTIST:

SONG:

PLAYLIST:

WHEN DID I STUDY?

MORNING

AFTERNOON

NIGHT

MY CLOSING PRAYER:

WHAT WAS HAPPENING IN MY LIFE?

WHAT WAS HAPPENING IN THE WORLD?

| MONTH | DAY | YEAR |

END DATE